As I Was Saying...

A Guide to the World of Competitive Speech
by: Thane Rehn

Published by
Communicators for Christ
www.CommForChrist.com
info@commforchrist.com
615-494-5023

Table of Contents

Introduction

"A word aptly spoken is like apples of gold in settings of silver." This proverb of King Solomon perfectly describes the joy that comes from a well-delivered speech. Public speaking is an art form in which the solid gold of form and content is enhanced by the silver of eloquence and elocution. Human beings are powerfully impacted by the effect of the spoken word and drawn to the beauty of well-woven communication.

This book is about competing in public speaking events. Competitive speech events offer the opportunity to practice and develop communications skills. There are a wide variety of speech events which are commonly referred to as individual events, or I.E.s for short. These can be narrowed down to three main categories: the platform speeches, the interpretive events, and the spontaneous or limited-preparation events.

First, a platform speech is written ahead of time by the student and delivered from memory. There are a wide variety of these with original oratory being the most popular. Oratory is a speech intended to persuade, entertain, or inspire the audience while expository speaking, another event, is designed simply to inform the audience and present important information about some subject. There are many other events as well, such as original advocacy, communication analysis, and after-dinner speaking. The common thread that unites all platform speaking

"Let your speech always be with grace, seasoned with salt, that you may know how you ought to answer each one."
- Colossians 4:6

5

is a speech composed by the student on whatever topic the student chooses, and delivered from memory. The platform speech allows the speaker to say something meaningful about a topic which is important to him or her and teaches the art of effective rhetoric.

The interpretive events, by contrast, are always someone else's words which are interpreted by the speaker. In these events, the student selects a piece of literature and presents it by portraying its characters and their actions. The central divide is between dramatic interpretation which focuses on serious scenes, and humorous interpretation which looks at the lighter side. Other events are duo interpretation which is an interpretation performed by two people, thematic interpretation which involves a variety of literary selections revolving around a common theme, and oratorical interpretation in which the speaker re-enacts a famous speech from history. Interpretive events are popular because they provide the opportunity to actually perform and entertain the audience.

The final category of competitive speech includes the two spontaneous events, impromptu and extemporaneous, which are almost completely different from each other. Impromptu speaking is the one speech event where the speaker actually prepares his or her speech in the presence of the audience and the judges. The speaker receives a topic and is given two minutes to prepare a five minute speech. Due to the severe limitation on preparation, each speaker must rely on his or her own knowledge.

Extemporaneous speaking, on the other hand, probably relies on more research than any other individual event. In an extemporaneous speech, the speaker receives a topic, which is always about current events, thirty minutes before delivering a seven minute speech on it. Speakers prepare extensively before tournaments to be ready to intelligently address any topic they might receive. Both of these limited-preparation events require students to be well-read and well-informed, organized, and smooth, eloquent speakers.

Before you proceed, you will probably want to know why in the world you would ever want to get involved in something like this. Individual events offer many benefits, and participation in these events produces articulate, interesting individuals who know how to defend what they believe. In addition, competitive public speaking teaches the self-confidence and communications skills that will be deeply beneficial to every other activity you ever undertake. These benefits explain why such a large percentage of former speech competitors have risen to leadership positions in politics, careers, and churches.

Honestly, however, the real reason most students begin competing in speech is that it is so much fun. Individual events offer something for everyone no matter what your interests are. From humorous interpretation to original oratory, and from expository speaking to impromptu, every individual event has its own special appeal. Furthermore, no other school activity will give you the same chance to let your voice be heard. In individual events, you have a remarkable amount of freedom to speak your mind, and have others listen to what you have to say. Many students relish this opportunity. Through speech competition, you will also gain many friends. Individual events are a great chance to have fun while pursuing your interests.

On a more lasting level, the skills learned through speech competitions are skills which you will carry with you throughout your life. The first of these is the ability to feel comfortable in front of an audience. Public speaking will force you to overcome the fear of embarrassment and become comfortable with presenting your own words to a group of people. This leads to perhaps the greatest benefit of the individual events; they teach you how to articulate and support your own world view and opinions. Many individual speaking events require the student to take a side on an issue, and explain that position to the observer. You will learn how to support your ideas and learn various methods you can use to convince an audience. Developing the ability to think for yourself and explain your ideas to others is of critical importance toward developing into some one who can impact those around you with the truth.

These may all be considered excellent reasons to participate in public speaking, but many students might still be wondering why they should actually go out there and compete. Competition raises the bar for everybody involved in any activity. It provides that extra incentive to try harder, put in more work, and do a better job. Students who have trouble staying motivated will be much more excited about preparing their speeches when there is a chance to win. In addition, getting ready for competition is a lot more fun than just writing a speech as an assignment for a club. Competition teaches you how to improve your speech by concentrating on a single speech throughout the season, refining it to communicate to as broad an audience as possible. Competition will give you more opportunities to deliver speeches, spur you on to fulfill your full potential, and allow you to have much more fun with speech than you would have had otherwise.

No element of human society would be possible without interpersonal communication, and the quality of that communication is of great importance to the health of society. The various individual events concentrate on different aspects of public communication. The platform speeches will prepare you to identify a problem and persuade others to change their attitude or actions in response, or to provide an accurate description of a pertinent issue. The interpretive events provide an artistic outlet in the fine art of performing, in addition to helping students understand how to relate to human emotions and represent the human condition. Finally, the spontaneous events help you to think on your feet, and quickly organize your thoughts in response to an important idea. All of these work together to create a complete picture of the various forms of oral communication, and will help you to become a more persuasive, eloquent, intelligent, and interesting person.

This is perhaps most apparent when one takes a look at some of those who became involved in individual events at a young age. Many of the most important communicators in our society have publicly praised the value of competitive speech in their own lives, a diverse group that includes Oprah Winfrey, Rush Limbaugh, and Ted Turner, among hundreds of others. When one considers the tremendous social impact just these three have had, the value of learning how to influence others becomes crystal clear. This world needs many Christians who can stand up and communicate the most important message, to be shining lights in an often dark world. The life skills imparted by competitive speech are invaluable tools toward realizing that possibility.

Part One: Platform and Limited Preparation Speeches

How to Write a Speech

There is something special about a speech. Public speaking has a unique power to move people in very powerful ways, and great public speakers have changed the course of world history time and time again. In order to harness the power of the spoken word, you need a special set of skills that are different from the skills required in any other form of communication. For example, good speakers are often good writers, but good writing does not necessarily translate into good speaking. A great piece of writing will often sound too complicated or boring when it is read aloud, while the wording of a spectacular speech might look overly repetitive or cumbersome on the printed page. This chapter will explain the working components of verbal communication, including speech form, style, and content. We will discuss what makes a speech effective, and learn about a basic structure that can be applied to any type of public speaking, prepared or spontaneous. The methods discussed in this chapter will give you the tools you need to become the most effective communicator you can possibly be.

Choosing a Topic

The first step in writing a speech is choosing a topic. There are many public speaking situations when the topic is chosen for you, such as when you are asked to give a presentation at work, or when a policeman pulls you over and asks you why you were driving so fast. In these cases, you simply have to do your best with the topic you have been given. In many other cases, however, you will have at least some input into the decision making process. For example, if you are preparing to give a speech at your church or do a spoken report for school, there are often some general guidelines about what you should talk about, but the specific topic is up to you.

There is only one rule when it comes to deciding on a topic for a speech: talk about what you care about. If you are like me, this means that there are many possible topics to choose from. I have given speeches about many different topics, including the miracles of Jesus, human rights, Dr. Seuss, and the value of public speaking. These different subjects have only had one thing in common, which was that I thought that they were important for one reason or another.

If you talk about a subject that you find boring, the audience will also find it boring because your lack of interest will show through. Even if you have been given a topic to speak on, it is vitally important that you find something in that topic that you care about. Always communicate your passion for what you are saying. If you can not find a reason to be passionate about it, then it is probably not be worth saying at all.

Before you get too involved in writing your speech, make sure you discuss your ideas with a few people. It is possible that you have some interests that the rest of the world finds completely boring. I know I do. You might think that your collection of pocket lint is the most fascinating thing in the world, but not very many people want to sit through a speech entitled "How to Collect Pocket Lint." A second thing to consider is whether or not your subject will be fresh for the audience. If something has been all over the news lately, for example, you might want to ask yourself if anyone really needs to hear another speech about it. You do not want your audience to feel like they have heard everything you have to say before.

Finally, consider how well this topic will keep your interest. Preparing a good speech takes a large amount of time and commitment, and you do not want to put all your hard work into something that will not be worth the effort. Think about how much research you will want to do for this topic, and whether or not there is really enough to say about it to warrant a speech.

It is not enough just to have a good idea what you are speaking about. After deciding on a topic, you need to get very specific and formulate what is known as a thesis. The thesis is the purpose of your speech, the main point that you want to get across. Think about whether you are trying to persuade the audience of something, to inform them about something, or to inspire them. Each of these requires a different thesis statement. I cannot emphasize too much that this is a thesis statement, not a thesis paragraph. You need to summarize the main point of your speech in one sentence, and if you are having trouble doing that, then you should refine your choice of topic. Clarity of purpose is essential to prevent a muddled, confusing speech, and a speech that tries to do too much will end up accomplishing nothing.

Form

Every single speech you deliver should have the same basic format. The fundamental structure of a speech contains three parts; the introduction, the body, and the conclusion. These are the parts that make up the outline of the speech. You should fashion every part of your outline in light of your thesis, to create a logical, progressive illumination of your topic. The outline form can be thought of as the skeleton of the speech. Like a body without a skeleton, a speech without a solid outline will be a formless blob, drooping, rambling, and incoherent, regardless of the amount of research you have done. The introduction, body, and conclusion must be clearly defined, and all three have to flow together, for the speech to connect with the audience.

Introduction: The introduction of the speech comes, appropriately, at the beginning. It is the audience's first impression of you, the speaker, and thus it is essential for you to get off to a good start. Studies of verbal communication show that if a speaker fails to grab the audience from the beginning, they will tune her out regardless of what she says or does from that point on. On the other hand, when a speaker can make a forceful first impression, the audience is predisposed to pay attention to her. The very first thing that you say in your speech should immediately arrest the attention of everyone listening. Speakers call this attention getter a hook.

Think about how you would go about catching a fish. You need a hook with a bright fly or a tasty worm on it, because the only way to get the fish is to attract its attention with something that it finds interesting. The hook is connected to your fishing pole, of course, so that you can use it to reel in your fish. This is exactly how your introduction should work on your audience. You need to grab their attention with something that is connected to the main point of your speech. If you can do this successfully, it will be easy to reel them in. Before you know it, you will have your audience scaled, gutted, and cooking in a frying pan. Well, maybe that is carrying the analogy a little bit too far, but you should keep the hook in mind when you write your introduction.

One of the best ways to begin your speech is with a joke or an amusing personal anecdote. If this is delivered well, and with a smile, you will win the audience over to you, and they will think of you as a likable, interesting speaker with whom they can relate. Some of the best audience responses come when the speaker relates a funny or embarrassing personal story. Regardless of your subject matter, a lighthearted introduction will establish the personal connection with the audience that every speaker needs.

If your taste runs to the dramatic, you might want to begin your speech with a very different sort of hook. One common example of a hook is the dramatic use of a shocking statistic. Instead of opening with "Today I would like to talk about crime," it is far more interesting to begin by telling the audience "By the time I finish this sentence, another person in America will be murdered." The purpose of this sort of introduction is to surprise the audience out of their complacency and get them emotionally invested in the speech right from the start.

You might also consider attempting to hold your audience in suspense for a short while before you let on what your speech will be about. Build up some anticipation and then surprise your audience with a little twist. For example, if you are giving a speech about your favorite painting, do not begin by saying "Today I would like to talk about the Mona Lisa." Instead, introduce your speech with this:

"I am in love with a woman who is six hundred years old. You may think that is crazy, but you might just fall for her too when you see her smile. I'm not the only one, because this lady has been admired by everyone from Louis XIV to Napoleon. Her name is the Mona Lisa."

Notice how this introduction works. The first sentence completely throws the audience for a loop, and they have no idea what the speaker is talking about. By keeping the audience in suspense, even for a short while, you will quickly engage them in your topic. This sort of introduction is easy to come up with, and will work for almost any topic.

A final common introduction style is the use of stories or quotations from history, literature, or current events. A tactic which adds instant weight and authority to your speech is to open with a ringing quotation from a famous personage. It's fascinating how this works. I have personally seen a joke fall flat on its face when simply told as if it were the speaker's own writing, only to see the same joke earn peals of laughter when attributed to someone such as Groucho Marx. An audience will likely be unimpressed by your assertion that "No government is better than the men who compose it." However, when they know that John F. Kennedy said that, you will find them nodding in agreement. Because of this quirk of human psychology, an introduction that quotes somebody whom the audience has heard of will be much more impressive than anything you write yourself.

Regardless of the hook you choose, the very first words out of your mouth should prepare everyone in the room to listen to what you have to say. This entails more than just getting their attention. The introduction is not used just to pull the listeners in, but it also becomes the hook on which you hang your entire speech. To do this, you need to have a smooth transition from the initial attention grabber into the flow of your speech. The ideas laid out at the beginning should become the backbone of your presentation. Use your hook to set up your thesis, and explain to the audience what you will be talking about over the course of your speech.

After establishing the thesis, tell the audience what to expect from the rest of your speech. In what is called a road map, lay out the major points and themes you will be addressing as you consider the topic. This lets the listeners know what to expect, and prepares them for your central ideas. After presenting the road map, you can transition into the meat of your speech, the body.

To summarize, the introduction is of extreme importance to your speech, as it allows you to make a strong first impression and lay the foundation on which to build the rest of the speech. To accomplish this, begin by capturing the audience's attention and sympathy with a strong hook which sets up your central thesis. Explain the thesis, or purpose of your speech, and then provide a clear road map which tells what ground your speech will cover. Together, these parts will create a smooth, interesting introduction and start you off on the right foot.

Body: The body of your speech is the place where you have to do all the hard work, laying out the facts and contentions that support your thesis. This is where organization becomes critical, to prevent your material from getting lost or confused in the minds of the audience. The tool for organization is simple, but beautiful - the outline. The most common outline is the three-point outline. To have the most memorable speech possible, you should organize your ideas into three main points, identify those points in the road map in your introduction, and then explain each one in detail during the body.

The consensus among the authorities is that three is the magic number, and that a speech just isn't any good without three main points. In my experience, this is usually true, and a three-point outline is often the most versatile and memorable way to organize your speech. If you promise not to tell my speech teacher from high school, however, I will confess that there have been times when I did not stick to the strict three-point outline. Sometimes my subject matter just would not fit into any less than five points, while other times I could cover my topic with two central ideas.

The important thing to keep in mind is not so much the number of points that you have, but that everything you say in your speech fits into some sort of outline. I have yet to see the speaker who can blow an audience away by just rambling disjointedly between ideas.

To select your main points, you should consider how to best support your thesis. Decide on the main reasons why you support your thesis, and place those at the center of your speech. Think about the logical flow of your ideas, and organize your thoughts along this flow. For example, if you are giving a persuasive speech, you could use your first point to make the audience aware of a problem. After this, in your second point you can talk about why the problem exists and why it is not likely to go away under present conditions. Finally, your third point can present a solution to the problem. This is the dominant form of outline used in academic debate, public policy discussion, and most business presentations.

Another common way of deciding on the major ideas that will support your thesis is to examine your topic from several different angles. Like the blind men feeling the elephant, everything looks different depending on what part of it you examine. Think about which angles will give your audience the most complete picture of your topic.

In a speech about the Mona Lisa, the first main point could discuss how this painting came to be and what went into its creation by Leonardo. After this, you could discuss the history of the painting and why it became so famous. Finally, you could examine the painting itself and discuss what makes it such a profound image. Each point adds a new layer to the understanding that the audience has.

Of course, every speech requires its own structure. If you are presenting the strategic vision for your company to the board of directors, you will probably want an outline that has meticulous logic, backed up by careful documentation and the appropriate facts and figures. If you are delivering the toast at your best friend's wedding, you probably just need a couple of stories that illustrate something about his or her character. Just remember that every speech will be made better if you put some serious thought into the structure you will use to present your ideas.

In conclusion, the body is the meat of the speech, providing the in-depth analysis and research that allows you to establish your thesis in the minds of the audience. One key to a successful speech lies in having a well-organized body with several carefully reasoned main points tied together by the common theme of a strong outline. Speeches without this outline invariably have a disjointed feel, rambling around without any real punch. The audience will only enjoy your speech to the extent they can follow and understand it. Shaky organization in the body causes the entire speech to crumble. As you write your speech, organize your research into a few main ideas designed to back up the thesis.

Conclusion: Let us conclude our discussion of speech form by saying a few words about the conclusion. Many speech conclusions are very poorly prepared, just a few afterthoughts tacked on to an otherwise strong speech simply for the sake of having an ending. As a result, many speeches have an unsatisfactory finish that says very little. This is not what you want your conclusion to be. A good conclusion should tie together all the previous parts of the speech and bring the main point of the speech into clear focus. After your speech has introduced a variety of facts, examples, and ideas, the conclusion should crystallize the picture, boiling everything down to extract the purpose of what has been covered. This can be done if your conclusion possesses three basic characteristics.

The first objective for a strong conclusion is to summarize and restate the main points of the speech. This means, if you have been following the advice in this chapter so far, your speech will lay out its main points in the introduction, explain and expound upon each of those points in detail during the body, and review all of them once again in the conclusion. While many students initially think of this as redundant, such repetition is actually a crucial component of getting your message across to the audience. When you are writing an essay, the reader is at leisure to go at her own pace and refer back to earlier points if something is unclear. During a speech, on the other hand, the audience only has one chance to hear what you tell them.

The human brain needs to hear an idea several times before it registers, as any advertiser could tell you, so make sure that the most important points in your presentation are restated more than once. An old public speaking mantra explains this idea well:

Tell them what you are going to tell them. Tell them. Tell them what you told them. Your conclusion is the final opportunity to make sure that the audience gets your message.

While you summarize your basic outline, you should also go back to your thesis and restate the central theme of your speech. If any aspects of your speech are potentially confusing, the conclusion is a good time to retrace your steps and explain exactly how your points support your thesis. Remember, when you deliver a speech, it is the first time the audience has ever heard it. Unlike you, they haven't studied the subject in depth, and they might need clarification of points that you take for granted. When in doubt, always err on the side of adding more review in the conclusion than you think is needed.

A second characteristic of a well-crafted conclusion is that it refers back to the introduction. If you did your job at the beginning of the speech, the introductory hook made a strong impact on the audience. Use that to your advantage. Bring the statistic, story, or quotation that you used back into the minds of the audience by mentioning it once again. This not only recaptures their initial emotional response, but it also gives your speech an overarching cohesiveness and provides a sense of completion as you finish. Additionally, the conclusion is a good time to reexamine what was said at the beginning in light of what has been learned during the speech.

This is an excellent way to transition to the third and final task your conclusion needs to accomplish. Leave something ringing in the audience's ears. You want to end on a high note where you give one final thought about your topic. I have seen too many excellent speeches that ended, in the words of T.S. Eliot, "not with a bang but a whimper." You want to make sure that your speech stays strong right to the end.

Never conclude a speech with some sort of anemic little sentence like "It's clear that the Mona

Lisa is a beautiful painting." This is nothing more than a boring statement of the obvious, making your speech appear to be an exercise in trivial banality. Rather, you want to close with a little bit more of a pop. Consider something like this:

"Not many women can dream of staying young and beautiful for centuries, but the Mona Lisa already has. The same smile that caught Leonardo's eye has earned countless admirers throughout history. She will still be laughing at us when my grandchildren have grandchildren of their own."

Notice that this says pretty much the same thing as the boring ending, just with a little bit more flash. Your audience will remember your speech a lot better if you put just a little bit more thought into your concluding sentences.

As you end, step back from your speech a little and explain how it applies to real life. Don't just restate your thesis one more time, but take that thesis and tell the audience how it affects them and what they should do about it. You might close with an eloquent quotation which summarizes what was said, or ask a provocative rhetorical question for the audience to consider, or anything else which gets them to remember your message. No matter what your topic, you should be able to summarize the point of your speech in a way that leaves the audience with something to think about. Make yourself absolutely clear what that is by finishing strongly with it.

A conclusion is not just ear candy or filler material thrown out at the end of your speech. It is an absolutely critical component of speech format without which any speech will be left dangling for the audience to interpret as they will. Every conclusion must provide a clear summary of what has been said, tie it all back into the introduction and thesis, and end on a strong note by presenting the overall message of the speech in some memorable way. When speaking, do not simply end. Be sure you conclude.

Content

As I mentioned above, the form of the speech is the skeleton, the basic structure that provides shape and direction to the overall speech. In keeping with this analogy, the actual content of the speech is the flesh, the real meat of what you are trying to say. Due to the wide diversity in types of speeches, the specific content will be different for each speech. Nevertheless, there are a few basic building blocks that are essential to almost every public speaking situation.

Story: The story is the bread and butter of the public speaker, the most important thing to get right and the part of the speech that will stick with your audience the longest. No matter the speech topic, a simple story will help you get your point across better than any other method. People relate to other people, and everybody loves to hear a story. It is very important for you to provide that emotional link so your audience will feel connected to what you are saying. In our day and age especially, statistics are meaningless. Everybody has them, and they can be used to support almost anything, it seems.

A story, on the other hand, will never lose its staying power. When giving a speech, it is your responsibility to find good stories that help to communicate your message. The more specific your story is, the better. Tell the audience the name of the person in your story and give as much background information as you can. The more real that your story seems, the better the audience will relate. This goes for all types of speeches, in all categories. There is always room for a good story.

The place to find good stories is usually through a little bit of research. Newspaper articles are full of them, and most good reporters know how to tell a story very well. It is also very effective to talk about your own life, using personal anecdotes to give life to your speech. Just think about the basic point you are trying to make and what type of story would work

"Speaking is for listening. Speeches are not effective when they are in the speaker's mind, in his notes on the lectern before him, or even when they are spoken aloud in the presence of an audience. Speeches become effective only as they are perceived in the minds of listeners."
- J. Jeffrey Auer

toward that end. All of us have had experiences in our life that have taught us lessons, and we can weave these life experiences into the stories that make up a good speech.

You can also use stories from books, movies, and - my favorite - children's literature. Holding your audience's attention with a story is a device that is as old as language itself. My favorite example of the power of a good story comes in the book of 2 Samuel, when the prophet Nathan confronts King David after the episode with Bathsheba.

If Nathan had been like most of us, he would have barged right in, pointing his finger and accusing David of his awful crime. Nathan knew better, however, and told David a story about a rich man who stole a precious lamb from a poor man. The story worked to provoke the king's emotions, and David got angry at the evil rich man in the story. It was only after this that Nathan made his larger point, that David was guilty of the same sort of crime. Every public speech should make the audience think differently, and Nathan dramatically demonstrated how effective a story can be.

Evidence and Examples: You are not a very credible person. I am not attacking you in particular, but simply pointing out that none of us really has the authority to give our own opinion about something and assume that will be enough. No speaker anywhere who just makes assertions will be trusted. At some point, no matter who you are, you will have to back up what you say, and this is especially true for teenagers, whom nobody thinks of as credible at all.

In order to overcome this credibility gap, you should have a wide variety of evidence and examples for your speech. Even the most renowned experts in the world rely on evidence when they speak, because it is always good to have someone else who agrees with you. Good speakers support their ideas with a careful presentation of the facts; bad speakers try to cover up the weakness of their ideas with lots of hot air and bluster.

Whatever you are talking about, you need to do your research. You want to be over prepared, to make sure that everything you say is beyond doubt. Trial lawyers put about ten days of work into every hour they spend in the courtroom, to ensure that they have a thorough understanding of their case. You might not need quite this much of a ratio, but you should always try to prepare yourself as completely as possible.

Research can manifest itself in the form of statistics, simple facts, and quotations from authorities. Your job is to present these in such a way that the audience finds you believable but not boring. Keep in mind that the purpose of presenting facts is to give your audience the information they need to understand your thesis. Do not overload your audience with more than they can handle, but keep your information crisp and to the point.

Use statistics sparingly, but be sure to use them when they support your ideas. Find the right statistics that provide an easy connection to the audience. Unless you are giving a speech at a Hollywood party, your audience is unlikely to ascribe much meaning to the exact number of kilograms of cocaine that are brought into this country every year. However, every audience will respond when you tell them that 87% of high school dropouts quit because of drug problems.

You are not delivering a peer-reviewed study for the New England Journal of Medicine, so you do not have to waste time providing the exact date, page number, research methods, and qualifications of every source you cite. It is helpful, on the other hand to let the audience know a little bit about where you are getting your information. "The New York Times reported last year that the Mona Lisa is worth 50 million dollars." If someone in your audience really wants more information about your sources, they can ask you after your speech.

Also remember that you shouldn't just spit facts out like watermelon seeds, but always provide some interpretation of them. Put your research into a straightforward framework that is interesting and supports your overarching point.

When delivering quotations, ask yourself why you need someone else to say something for you. Don't quote your neighbor or your younger brother, in other words. Usually quotations are used when a well known person has said something that benefits the speaker's viewpoint. The best quotations are short, hard-hitting, and memorable, like Patrick Henry's "Give me liberty or give me death." These statements, when attributed to someone with whom the audience is familiar, pack quite a punch and provide you with instant credibility. In some cases, it will be necessary to quote longer passages from magazines, newspapers, and other published sources, in order to establish some important information. This is usually not advisable, however, and you should use long quotations sparingly. Other people's words should be an enhancement, not the substance of your speech.

The final issue to consider as you incorporate evidence is the ethical standard. The rule is rather simple. Never misrepresent a statistic, quotation, or story. If a story is fictional, make it clear that it is fictional. If you do not know the author of a quotation, do not attribute it to someone. The reason for this is that it is misleading, dishonest, and wrong, and undermines the very purpose of communication. Not only that, but when it is discovered, it will permanently damage your credibility.

Humor: This is important. Every single speech should have some humor in it, regardless of topic or setting. No one expects you to be a stand up comedian, but your audience will deeply appreciate it if you give them something to smile about in the midst of a long speech. This is because people really like to laugh, and causing them to laugh will instantly endear you to any audience. If they are laughing with you, even if they are laughing at you, they will be much more attentive and interested in your message. Therefore, you should make a genuine effort to put one or two laugh moments into your speech.

Laughter can come from a joke, a funny story from your own experience, a clever quotation, or even a simple play on words. Feel free to borrow freely from television, books, and other speakers, as long as you remember to give credit where credit is due. A joke is especially effective when it makes your point in a humorous way.

Many people are nervous about public speaking, and they get that unavoidable nervous feeling in their stomach beforehand, kind of like the feeling you get from eating a half dozen live moths. In fact, a survey recently revealed that public speaking is the number one fear of most people. The number two fear is the fear of death. This means, as Jerry Seinfeld has pointed out, that if you go to a funeral, most people would rather be the guy in the casket than the guy up there giving the eulogy.

Jokes are a great way to relieve this tension. Smile, be light, and don't be afraid to make fun of yourself. Your audience will sympathize with you and you will have even more credibility. This goes for every kind of speech, and I have never seen a time where a little bit of humor was not appropriate. I have given speeches about little children being sold into slavery in which I opened with a joke. No audience in the world wants to feel bludgeoned to death by what you are saying, so give them a chance to relax every now and then.

Every speech you will ever give requires evidence in some form. The accurate presentation of facts, examples, and quotations makes for a far more interesting and believable presentation, and the use of a good story will stick with your audience for a long time. You should never leave out a few jokes, as well. As you craft your speech, you want to do intensive research on your topic so that you can employ all of these components of strong speech content. Always back up what you say.

Style

Every speaker should develop his or her own personal style, and every speech topic requires a slightly different approach. However, there are certain general stylistic rules you should always consider when writing a speech. It is very easy to bore an audience when you are talking to them for an extended period of time, so you should use every tool at your disposal to create a presentation that crackles with energy and can really take hold of an audience. This section will give some thoughts and ideas to help you prevent audiences from dozing off mid-presentation.

Writing: Your speech will sink like a crippled dolphin if the writing sounds at all unnatural or forced. Unless your speech sounds natural and conversational, the audience will tune you out almost instantly. While much of this is accomplished through delivery, the way the speech is written is of equal importance. This is because there is a huge difference between writing for the eye and writing for the ear.

When you write an essay or anything meant to be read, you have certain luxuries. The reader will be going at her own pace and can retrace your steps whenever she pleases. This is not so when you speak. The speech will go at the speaker's pace, and once something has been said, it is over, and the listener is unable to review it again. Long, complicated sentences (with parenthetical remarks), and elaborate sentence structure featuring several different clauses contained within the overall ebb and flow of the sentence, a flow which must be preserved regardless of other considerations, such as the desire to add more information, or further expand on a point, are anath-

Sidebar: Rhetorical Devices

There are many tools you can use to make your language more powerful. Here are some of the best:

1: Antimetabole
This is the repetition of certain words, but in reverse order.
"Ask not what your country can do for you, ask what you can do for your country."
- John F. Kennedy

2. Parallelism
Putting together phrases with similar sound and meaning.
"We shall pay any price, bear any burden, meet any hardship, support any friend, oppose any foe to assure the survival and success of liberty."
- John F. Kennedy

3. Anadiplosis
Beginning a sentence with the same words that came at the end of the previous sentence.
"This means much more than the mere success of a party. The success of a party means little except when Nation is using that party for a large and definite purpose."
- Woodrow Wilson

4. Restatement
The repetition of an important sentence several times in the course of a speech.

ema to a coherent speech. Actually, they usually do not add much clarity to your writing, either, but that is another issue. In a speech, try to rely on relatively simple, straightforward sentences, just like you would in ordinary conversation.

One of my favorite public speaking stories of all time provides a good illustration of the difference between speaking and writing. Winston Churchill, when informed by one of his speechwriters that he should not end sentences with prepositions, angrily retorted, "This is exactly the kind of nonsense up with which I don't have the time to put!" This is a perfect example of the important speech principle that the most important goal is to write in a style that sounds natural and pleasant to the ear, not stilted or artificial.

Vocabulary: Furthermore, be very careful about your vocabulary. Ask yourself whether you would ever actually use a word in normal conversation before using it in your speech. While you do want your writing to be clear and precise, it is certain that you will not impress an audience by using words they do not understand. Speakers who attempt to sound intelligent by filling their material with highfalutin, twenty-four dollar words always sound either confusing or, worse, foolish when they inevitably mispronounce or misuse words which were only added for dramatic effect.

Also, certain words and phrases just sound wrong. Speakers call these words undeliverable, and "undeliverable" is a great example of a word that is very difficult to use in a speech; it would probably come out as "undeliverabubble." If I were writing this chapter to be spoken instead of to be read, I would probably use "difficult to say" instead of "undeliverable." Pay close attention to elements in your speechwriting which could cause distraction when spoken, such as accidental alliteration and unnatural rhythms. Ask yourself if you will be able to recite your speech without it tripping up your tongue too much. If not, then rewrite those passages that are causing problems.

Pay very close attention to the connotation and possible interpretations of your words. I might refer to my grandmother as "plump," but I would never use "obese." As Mark Twain observed, "The difference between the right word and almost the right word is like the difference between the lightning and the lightning-bug." When in doubt, go with the easier word. For example, use "steadfast" but never use "indefatigable." Remember, write your speech as if you were talking to someone, not writing for someone.

If you are giving a speech about a technical subject, do not use too much jargon. If you are using a term that the audience might not be completely familiar with, take the time to explain what you are talking about. You want to communicate with your audience, not impress them with how smart you are.

Transitions: The transitions between your main points should accentuate and not interrupt your speech. Jumping from point to point with no linking material will make you sound as if you are reciting an outline, not delivering a speech. Look for the logical flow between your ideas and incorporate that into the transitions between the different parts of your speech. As you go from point to point, take a sentence or two to summarize what you have just said and explain how it links to what you are about to say.

Transitions are easy to do, but many speakers forget to use them. The important thing to keep in mind is to always make sure that your ideas are linked together and that the different parts of your speech sound like they fit together. Using parallel sentence structure can work very well as a transition, such as "Not only (point A), but also (point B)" and "In addition to (point B), we can see that (Point C)". The use of contrast is another way to transition from point to point. "We have seen the historical importance of this, but we should not forget that it is still in use today." You can also segue between ideas by just telling the audience what you are doing in your speech. "Now that we have covered our first area of analysis, let's move on to the next point in today's speech." Any of these sentences allow you to move seamlessly from point to point.

Indeed, even little words like "indeed" will help to polish your presentation. Use "furthermore" and "moreover." They don't really mean anything, but they make you sound more organized and provide a simple way to connect ideas. Try to make your speech as silky smooth as possible, so the audience is not distracted by poor phrasing and abrupt shifts in the focus. The words you use are simply a window through which the audience can see your ideas, and you want that window to be as clean and unobtrusive as possible.

In the final analysis, the way your speech is written must not interfere with what you are trying to say. Only use language you are comfortable with, because you are the one who will have to deliver it again and again. Do not ever artificially employ words simply to impress, and watch out for language that seems cumbersome when spoken. Polish off your speech by using crisp, clear transitions, and eliminate any wording that could distract the audience from the main point.

Re-writing: The secret to good writing is in the re-writing. Not a single person in the world is capable of writing her best possible work on the first draft. Every speech you write will be better after you have carefully read over it and tried to improve upon it. After you finish the first draft of your speech, you should leave it alone for a while, at least overnight. This is so it will be fresh for you when you begin to edit it. Spend some time reading the speech aloud, thinking about how it sounds and whether or not your message is clear.

You want to ask yourself very direct and specific questions about the speech, such as "How well do I transition from my third point to my conclusion?"

and "Is my explanation of the evidence sufficient in my first point, or will the audience have trouble following it?" Get into the details, the nuts and bolts that actually hold your speech together. This is the only way to effectively improve the writing of a speech.

This does sound like a lot to look out for, and you will probably discover how difficult it is to edit your own writing. Have somebody else look over your work as well. They will be able to give better feedback about whether the audience will be able to understand what you are saying. You would not

Delivery

In any public speech, the style and strength of delivery is as much a part of presentation as the actual writing of the speech. One of the most important delivery skills can not be taught, and that is to always let your own unique personality shine through. Each individual is different, and different styles work for different people. Your audience will appreciate it if you can just be yourself in front of them.

"The language of words is only a fragment of the language we use in communicating with each other. We talk with eyes and hands, with gestures, with our posture, with various motions of the body."
- Andrew Halpin

This does not mean that there are no guidelines for delivery. Certain aspects of delivery are universal and are used by every effective communicator. Public speaking is a whole body experience, not just a matter for your mouth. This section will go through some of the different body parts that are used when speaking before an audience, and how to use them.

Nerves: Without a doubt, the toughest thing to control when you are giving a speech is your nerves. While there are a few individuals out there who experience no stage fright whatsoever, they are the exception. I have given literally hundreds of speeches before large audiences in my life, and I still get the classic symptoms, including a pounding heartbeat, sweaty palms, and trembling hands.

You will never completely get over the inevitable butterflies that come with public speaking, but you do not have to succumb to them. You can increase your confidence by practicing ahead of time so that you are familiar with what you will say. At the beginning of your speech, try focusing on one familiar face in the audience and pretend that you are talking only to that person. Once you get on a roll, your nerves will disappear.

Also, it is a good idea to eliminate possible distractions that might reinforce your fears. If you know your hands will be trembly, do not carry papers that will rustle and draw attention. Use a lectern or deliver your speech without notes. Use notes that are typewritten in a large clear font. Think about your audience and not about yourself, and focus your energy on getting your message across.

"If you think you can win, you can win. Faith is necessary to victory."
- William Hazlitt

The real key to maintaining your self-confidence is to believe in your message. If you do not think you have anything worthwhile to say, the audience will agree with you. However, if you believe that you have a very important message which needs to be heard, the audience will sit up and take notice. Confidence should be manifested in several ways. From the moment you walk to the front of the room, you should be in complete control. Smile, speak clearly and with a calm demeanor, and stand still. Do not fidget or sway back and forth, but have a firm posture, and only move your hands and body when you have a reason to do so. Even if you have a memory lapse or verbal stumble, never look angry or embarrassed, and, above all, do not apologize to the audience. Chances are, they will hardly notice it if you do not call attention to it.

Voice: You want to speak in as clear and confident a voice as you can muster. If the audience can not understand you, you might as well be speaking a foreign language, so articulate your words. You should never deliver a speech while chewing gum. You should also remove any tongue rings, chewing tobacco, and peanut butter from your mouth well in advance of standing before an audience.

To further strengthen delivery, the rate at which you speak should be considered. The general tendency for speakers is too talk too rapidly, especially when they are nervous, making it difficult for the audience to follow them. I have almost never heard anyone speak too slowly. Calm yourself, speak naturally, and adopt a conversational tone. You are more likely to be understood and less likely to trip over your own words if you just talk naturally.

One of your best weapons as a public speaker is the well-timed pause. Try this sometime. Just stop yourself mid-sentence while talking and wait a beat before finishing your thought. This breaks up the monotony of your voice and instantly captures audience attention by building expectation for what you are about to say. Many speakers are afraid of the pause and rush to fill it with a verbalization, such as "um," "uh," "you know," or even clearing the throat. Fight this impulse, and allow yourself the occasional pause.

"The right word may be effective, but no word was ever as effective as a rightly timed pause."
- Mark Twain

Be sure to vary your tone, pitch, and volume, and avoid the steady monotone that will encourage audience members to head down the hallway for a coffee refill. I have accomplished some of my most elaborate doodling on the back of napkins during boring speeches, while the speaker's voice droned on in the background like a pesky fly. Use inflection, speak loudly enough that everyone can hear you without straining, and convey a genuine enthusiasm for your message.

Eyes: The single most important physical thing to do during your speech is to make as much eye contact as you can. A ten minute speech should feature about nine minutes and fifty-five seconds of direct eye contact with the audience. The eyes are an incredible tool, capable of sweeping a crowd and instantly locking onto one person, leaving no doubt as to whom they are focusing on. Unless you are speaking to an audience of several thousand, you should be able to make eye contact that is so precise that any audience member can tell when you are looking right at him. The most surefire way to keep someone paying attention to you is to capture his eyes.

This is why great public communicators from Elvis Presley to Ronald Reagan have had one common characteristic. They were capable of making individual audience members believe that they were talking directly to them. Direct eye contact is the chief means of connection with an audience, making them feel important and appreciated. No one wants to listen to a speaker who ignores his or her presence, so recognize the listener with your eyes.

One of the many benefits of eye contact is that it generates feedback through which you can evaluate how well your message is getting across. When you are in direct contact with the audience, you will be able to tell whether they are bored, confused, emotionally involved, or amused. Use the reactions that your audience gives you to make your delivery more effective. Eye contact shows that you are better prepared, confident, and truly sympathetic with your audience. Weak eye contact always separates the speaker from the listener and acts as a significant obstacle to communication.

Yet many speakers have great trouble maintaining eye contact. Some speakers look at the ceiling, the floor, or the back wall, which makes them look as if they are unsure of what to say, or they are just talking to themselves. Others do scan the audience with their eyes, but their gaze never actually settles on someone for the purpose of communication. When you make eye contact, pick one person to focus on for several seconds, then move on to another individual person to concentrate on. Over the course of your speech, engage many members of your audience, making them feel as if you are speaking to them and them alone.

Hands: There is no doubt that hands are good things to have. Imagine trying to shuffle cards without them. While giving a public speech, however, they often seem like more trouble than they are worth. If you find yourself fidgeting with your hands while speaking in front of an audience, you are not alone. One reason so many movies feature cigarette smoking is that it gives the actors something to do with their hands. In your case, it is probably not an option to light up during your speech, so you will need to exercise a little bit more self-control.

The important thing to remember when using your hands is that all movement should be purposeful. Your default position during your speech should be to stand with your arms hanging comfortably at your sides. If there is a lectern, you may also stand with your hands resting on it. Never hold your hands behind your back, like you are hiding something, or in front, like you are Adam or Eve. Do not put hands in pockets or play with hair or jewelry. This will distract the audience. Many speakers find themselves rubbing their hands together or picking at their clothing, all of which signals to an audience that you are nervous or poorly prepared.

When you use gestures, you should raise your arms well above the waist and use them to emphasize a particularly important point. Do not ineffectively wave your hands from below the belt, but make your gestures highly visible and pointed. When you are in front of an audience, you need to communicate that they are extremely important to you, so use gestures to draw them in, and eliminate any distracting uses of your hands.

One of the most disastrous uses of hands in a public speaking situation happened during one of the debates between George Bush the Elder and Bill Clinton. Bush was caught on camera several times checking his watch, signaling an utter disregard for the audience. Meanwhile, Clinton was a master of animated delivery, using his hands to emphatically make points and also to reach out to the audience. It would not be entirely inaccurate to say that Bush lost the election because of a distracting gesture, and because he forgot the crucial rule that every public speaker must remember. The audience comes first.

"Nor do not saw the air too much with your hand, thus; but use all gently, for in the very torrent, tempest, and (I may say) whirlwind of your passion, you must acquire and beget a temperance that may give it smoothness."
- Shakespeare

Posture: Your posture while speaking should also communicate your confidence and care for the audience. This means that you should balance your weight evenly, with your feet about shoulder-length apart. Do not sway back and forth like a willow tree on a windy day. Also, cure yourself of the chained elephant syndrome where you lift one leg and then the other without going anywhere. Try to be as comfortable as possible, without getting nervous or jumpy.

Some speakers roam around the stage like a strutting rooster, working out their nervous energy with constant walking while speaking. Others root themselves in one spot like they have been nailed there. The ideal is to find a happy medium between these two, walking only a few times over the course of your presentation. Move purposefully and confidently, from one fixed point on the stage to another. Walking can be used to indicate a transition in your speech, as you pause after one important point, walk a few steps, and resume speaking from your new position. You want this to appear natural and spontaneous. This is especially important if you are speaking from behind a lectern. You should definitely move out from behind it at least once, to demonstrate more of a connection with your audience.

Dress: Unless you are speaking to a nudist convention, your audience will get their first impression of you by the way you are dressed. I have always hated this reality, but the fact is that you are responsible for the image you convey with your clothes. You should dress to demonstrate that you respect your audience, keeping in mind that you want to appear credible and appropriate. In most cases, this means that you should dress professionally. Avoid wearing clothes that are distracting, such as an overly short skirt or a tie with big cartoon characters on it. Your words should make a statement that your clothes should not contradict.

You should try to look your best, but also dress appropriately for your audience. I would not wear a three piece suit when speaking before a junior high summer camp. Remember that you want your audience to feel important, which means that you should eliminate cellular phones, pagers, and other electronic devices. Don't just turn them off, but make sure you keep them out of sight. I always leave these items behind when I am speaking, because I want the audience to be the most important thing in the world at that moment.

As you can see, delivering a speech is indeed a full body activity. You should put careful thought into every aspect of your presentation, and incorporate the right steps to make yourself appear confident and comfortable in front of an audience. Reach out to your audience with your voice, your ayes, and your hands, using your own personality and style to win them over. The end result should be a complete presentation, a speech that achieves a perfect fusion of form, content, and delivery, and moves the audience in a special way.

Practice: Like every performance, a successful speech relies on lots of practice. You should definitely run through your speech once or twice before the real thing, to prepare yourself and reinforce your confidence. Plan ahead where you will incorporate pauses, how you will tell stories and jokes, and what the emotional high points of your speech will be. Think about the flow of your ideas, and what style of presentation would be best. If possible, you should run through your speech at least once in front of a friendly audience, to get some advance feedback about what works and what does not. Put enough preparation into your speech so that you can feel completely ready when the time comes to actually deliver it.

After writing your speech for the purpose of being spoken, you should carefully refine the way you speak it. Certain elements of delivery are absolutely essential to the success of all speeches. Eye

"All the great speakers were bad speakers at first."
- Ralph Waldo Emerson

contact, confidence, and the appropriate use of gesture and voice should all be practiced and incorporated into your own personal speaking style. The end result should be a complete presentation, a speech that achieves a perfect fusion of form, content, and delivery, and moves the audience in a special way.

Original Oratory

You have your own absolutely unique perspective on the world. This includes experiences you have had, lessons you have learned, people in your life who have been important to you, the things that you care about, the things that you want, and the things that you dislike. In your life, you will want to share your perspective with other people; this sharing is what communication is all about. Society relies on good clear communication between people, and it is extremely important for each of us to learn how to share our ideas and thoughts with others.

Public speaking is one of the best ways to gain strong communication skills, and an original oratory is a public speech in it most pure form. In an original oratory, you get to decide on a topic that you feel is important enough to spend some time sharing about, a message that you want to communicate to an audience. To do this, you will research, write, and deliver a speech, crafting your words to deepen the audience's understanding and appreciation of your ideas. Original oratory will make you a better communicator, enhance your people skills, and help you to feel comfortable and confident when sharing your thoughts with others, even complete strangers.

These are important benefits that original oratory will give you, but the real benefit of oratory is that it teaches you to harness the power of the spoken word. The world desperately needs strong

"A speech is poetry: cadence, rhythm, imagery, sweep! A speech reminds us that words, like children, have power to make dance the dullest beanbag of a heart."
- Peggy Noonan

Christians who are willing to boldly communicate the good news. Not only will strong communication skills help you in your own life, but they will also increase your ability to be an active witness to God's glory.

How it Works in Competition

An original speech must be a speech that is written by the individual giving the speech, and it provides a student with the most pure possible forum for proclaiming her own ideas. This event will help to make you more comfortable and confident with your own ideas, and teach you how to articulate opinions as forcefully and persuasively as possible. Everyone has ideas and opinions, but it is those who can best present those ideas who are able to produce social change. The event of original oratory will teach you to craft words for the presentation of your world view.

In competition, an oratory must be completely scripted word for word. The range of topics is very broad. Your speech can alert the audience to a problem, offer an uplifting or thought-provoking message, strengthen devotion to a cause, pay tribute to an individual, or encourage the audience to be better people. A speech can be intended to persuade, to inform, to inspire, or to entertain. You are only allowed to include up to 150 words of direct quotation from outside sources, but aside from that there are few limitations. The purpose of oratory is to allow you to communicate the message you want to communicate.

Preparing an Original Oratory

Topic Selection: To prepare an original oratory, you first want to decide on a topic to discuss. This is entirely determined by your interests and passions. A good topic could be a lesson that you have learned in your own life. If you have had some recent experiences that have dramatically affected you, you can probably weave these into the backbone of a strong persuasive speech. You can talk about the importance of trusting in God, or the value of trying new things. Using examples from your own life to explain how you have learned and grown is a good way to connect with an audience. In many cases, a topic like this will lead to a speech that inspires the audience or broadens their perspective on life.

The more personal that you get, the more your speech will connect to the audience. A good oratory might discuss the special meaning of a family Christmas to the speaker, or it might share how the speaker has dealt with a personal tragedy or hardship. If you are willing to open up and be vulnerable before an audience, you can break through and achieve truly meaningful communication.

The topic you choose does not have to be inspirational or extremely personal in the normal sense. You might simply want to convince your audience to drink eight glasses of water every day or drive more cautiously. If you have an idea to share, then it can definitely be the subject of a good speech. Again, always choose a topic that is valuable to you but also practical and helpful for the people who you will be talking to.

"Nothing is so unbeliev-able that oratory cannot make it acceptable."
- Cicero

Yet another popular way to choose a speech topic is to work an entire speech around a single theme. For example, a friend of mine once wrote an extremely powerful original oratory based on the hymn "Amazing Grace." He wove together several stories and Biblical principles into a discussion of the message of this hymn. Another effective speech that I have seen was a discussion of the life of the evangelist Charles Fuller, who started Fuller Seminary. The speaker used examples from Fuller's life to illustrate a few basic lessons that she wanted to convey.

Some speakers want nothing more than to entertain the audience, and this is perfectly acceptable as well. You can tell a string of amusing anecdotes about your family, or share some of your more embarrassing moments. You can create a speech by weaving together a group of funny or unusual observations about a common subject or area of society. This is often referred to as an after-dinner speech, because it might be the sort of speech one is expected to give at a polite dinner party.

A broad topic area is not enough for a successful speech. As we discussed in the "How to Write a Speech" section of this book, you need to make sure that you boil down your speech topic to a very specific thesis. You want the thesis to be straightforward, simple, and easy to remember. Every other part of your speech should be designed to establish your thesis in the minds of the audience. A good thesis is a memorable and interesting message that the audience can take away from your speech.

Preparation: Once you have decided on your topic and written a strong thesis, you want to do some thorough research to gain an in depth knowledge of your topic. The type of research that you do will vary widely depending on your style of topic. You may need to obtain a large variety of statistics and background information from recent issues of newspapers and magazines if your topic revolves around current events. If you are giving a speech along spiritual or inspirational themes, you will probably want to read what the Bible and other great thinkers have to say about your topic. Other speech topics may require that you read or at least skim through a few books on the topic to get more information.

You want to begin organizing your research into a strong outline. Again, remember what we have said about speech outlines in the speechwriting chapter. You want an attention-getting introduction that leads into your thesis, a few main points that support your thesis, and a conclusion that wraps everything up well and ensures that the thesis of your speech will be stuck in the mind of the audience. Use what you know about your topic to organize your thoughts in a way that will be easy to follow and remember.

After you have written your outline, you should begin filling in your speech with strong examples and illustrations. Remember that everything you say should support your main point, and that it is your job to make the connections for your audience. Your main point, or your thesis, should be completely obvious to your audience; it should be a one sentence message that you especially emphasize time and time again. It has been said that the reason it is called the main point is that you should be able to point to it on the written manuscript of your speech. On a good speech, you should be able to point to it several times.

This is especially true of a speech, but it is also true of any form of communication. An excellent example of emphasizing a single main point is in the movie Spider-Man. The thesis of that movie was clear to everyone who watched it: "With great power comes great responsibility." the screenwriters did a very good job of bringing that simple concept out several times over the course of the film. Your speech should do the same with whatever your central message is.

Final Touches: Write your speech using the techniques that are covered in the chapter on speech writing. After writing it, remember to practice it again and again, refining your presentation and using the comments of others to make improvements. The ultimate goal of an original oratory is to have a speech that effectively communicates your personality and enables you to connect to an audience with your own ideas.

Persuasive Speaking

All around you, 24 hours a day, you are surrounded by messages of persuasion. From Madison Avenue to Hollywood, from Washington D.C. to your next door neighbor, just about everyone has an opinion and is eager that you share it. The basic goal of persuasive speech is to change the attitudes and actions of an audience, and this has never been a more difficult or a more valuable thing to do than it is today. It is difficult and valuable because of the sheer volume of persuasive speech going on.

I recently watched a political speech on television that illustrated this. The speaker spoke, frequently interrupted by a team of news commentators. This was followed by a discussion between a panel of political analysts, and then by an official rebuttal to the initial speech, given by a politician from another party. The main news anchor concluded the program with some thoughts of his own. Of course, the entire parade of opinions was punctuated with a stream of commercials that endlessly contradicted each other about which soft drinks, fast foods, and toothpastes I should be using.

In a world filled with powerful tools and amazing new technologies, the simple techniques of persuasion that are discussed in this chapter are still the most valuable instruments known to humankind. The power of persuasion is what changes the course of individual lives and therefore the overall flow of events in the world. There is no limit to what it can

"With public sentiment, nothing can fail; without it, nothing can succeed. Consequently he who molds public sentiment goes deeper than he who enacts statutes or pronounces decisions."
- Abraham Lincoln

accomplish. As evidenced by such figures as Martin Luther King, Ronald Reagan, and Billy Graham, the transforming power of a persuasive speech is truly inestimable.

How it Works in Competition

"The wise in heart will be called discerning, and sweetness of speech increases persuasiveness."
- Proverbs 16:21

If you are like most people, you have developed a few beliefs of your own, but you often feel like you do not have a chance to express them. With so many voices clamoring for attention, not many of us have a real chance to stand up and be heard. The competitive individual event of Persuasive Speaking gives you that chance. In this event, you are asked to write and deliver a ten minute speech about any topic you desire. Many students enjoy their first experiences with oratory, and are excited about the opportunity to share their own unique perspectives on issues that are important to them. If you have an opinion about something and you have always wanted to share it, then oratory is the perfect event for you.

Not only does oratory provide a soapbox, but it will also train you how to use that soapbox in the most persuasive way possible. Through participating in oratory, students learn to communicate what they believe and why they believe it, and how to win over hostile audience members with charm, conviction, and careful reasoning. Whether you choose to propose a solution to a problem, encourage certain actions or beliefs, draw attention to an important issue, or inspire your audience to be better people in some way, you will have to craft your words with precision and thoughtfulness, and do your best to produce change in the hearts and minds of the listeners. Persuasion is a difficult but important task.

In competition, a persuasive speech can fit into a range of categories. Some speech leagues lump together all persuasive speeches into the broad category of original oratory, while others form two or three separate categories. In some leagues, there is a category known as original advocacy in which the

48

speaker is asked to focus on a problem in the world of current events and then propose a solution that would be enacted as a law or government policy. Persuasive speaking can also be expanded to include any speech that the speaker gives that is intended to persuade the audience how to think or act on a specific issue.

Preparing a Persuasive Speech

Topic Selection: To prepare a persuasive speech, you first need to find something that you care about. It is impossible to prepare an effective speech about something that you are not personally interested in. Thus, as you try to find a topic, you should think about things that are important to you. Maybe you have observed a problem in society that you think ought to be addressed. This could be a very tangible problem, such as pollution, or something intangible like greed. You may want to address this problem and propose a solution. A common type of speech is one in which the speaker advocates for a new law or policy to address a problem in society.

If you do choose to lay out a specific policy proposal or official course of action for the government to take, you should focus on convincing your audience to believe strongly in the value of your idea. You may want to encourage the audience to take action, such as contacting their Congressman or becoming active in support of a cause. You should always make sure that the major focus of a persuasive speech should be to influence the actions or beliefs of your audience. Do not try to persuade them to do something that they are unable to do, but try to give some specific and practical ways that the people who are likely to hear your speech can do something about it.

Tools of Persuasion

There are three components to the presentation of a good persuasive oratory. Aristotle referred to these as ethos, pathos, and logos. In modern English, the three parts of persuasion are the speaker's credibility, the emotional appeal to the audience, and the logic and reasoning that are used to back up what the speaker says.

Ethos: You establish your ethos, or your credibility, by a number of things. You should speak confidently and look the audience in the eye. Demonstrate a full knowledge of your topic and make sure that you have prepared and practiced your speech as much as possible.

The delivery for a persuasive speech should be natural and conversational, but occasionally fired with intense conviction and passion for your message. Choose the emotional high points ahead of time, and emphasize those when speaking. Be passionate, but be real. The audience will see through any attempt to be artificially eloquent and intelligent sounding or to be emotionally cloying and manipulative. Resist the urge to dress up your subject. Treat it genuinely and approach your speech as sincerely and candidly as possible in order to establish your credibility.

Pathos: The concept of pathos, or emotional appeal, comes primarily from your use of good stories and illustrations. People will forget most of what you say fairly quickly, as you can demonstrate next Monday evening by trying to reconstruct the outline of your pastor's Sunday sermon. A good story, on the other hand, sticks with an audience. You should always weave several anecdotes into your speech, anecdotes that are drawn from news stories, history, or your own life. The latter are some of the best, because you will be at your best when you are sharing about yourself.

A good story usually revolves around one main character or the relationship between two main characters. The characters should learn something or achieve something, and the story should provoke a clear reaction from the audience. Some times this reaction should be laughter, some times it should be tears, and other times you need a story that is uplift-

"Three things matter in a speech; who says it, how he says it, and what he says – and, of the three, the last matters the least."
- John Morley

50

ing or inspiring. The best speeches use all of these types of stories.

In a ten minute speech, you should have two or three good stories at the least, introducing one every three minutes or so. Audience attention spans are short, and you will tend to lose your audience if you do not give them examples, illustrations, and anecdotes frequently. In order to strike a strong emotional chord for the audience to latch onto, you should support your main point with stories.

Pathos is especially important if you are speaking on a topic that demands a response of pity or compassion from the audience. Many problems in the world are extremely tragic, and it is often the role of the public speaker to alert people to these tragedies. If you want to inspire a genuine change of heart on the part of your audience members, which is the ultimate goal of persuasion, you need to appeal to their heart.

I once gave a speech about the problem of children being sold into slavery in certain areas of the world. In my speech, I presented a large amount of statistics and documentation to prove the existence of the problem. I also stated strongly that this is a serious and terribly sad problem that is too often ignored. None of my evidence or assertions, however, worked to win over the audience. In order to do that, I simply had to share a few stories and details about what happens to children in slavery. I had to talk about some uncomfortable issues, such as beatings and abuse of children as young as five years old.

These stories were what won over the audience every time. As I delivered the speech, I could watch the emotional impact of my descriptions playing out in the facial expressions of the audience members. It was not the quality of the evidence or the fervency of my beliefs that won them over, but their compassionate response to the issues I was discussing. This is the essence of pathos, and it demonstrates how important it is to provide the audience with a strong set of emotional images to react to. People are moved by their hearts more than their brains.

Logos: The final aspect of persuasion is the logos, which is the actual logic and reasoning that you use to support your ideas. This comes from solid documentation of any facts that you introduce, and an outline that flows reasonably from point to point. One helpful tactic as you write your speech is to tell a few people what the purpose of your speech is and ask them for the first objection that pops into their head. It is a safe bet that your audience will have the same sort of objection when you deliver your speech, so provide an answer for it. You want to appear very credible, and a careful analysis of possible disagreements to your point will be much more persuasive than ignoring those disagreements.

To strengthen the logical appeal of your speech, make sure that everything you say is ultimately intended to provide support to your central thesis. Just as every column of a Greek building is intended to hold up the roof, so every point in your speech should be intended to hold up your message before the audience. Do not hope for your audience to make the connections between your ideas. It is your responsibility to ensure that every point is explained clearly. Take the time to tell the audience how each argument, illustration, and piece of evidence that you present is linked to the overall purpose of your speech.

This means that your main point will be continually brought before the minds of the audience. The repetition and restatement of your message several times provides a strong sense of unity to your speech and gives it a deep and persuasive resonance with the listeners. Use this to your advantage and never miss an opportunity to drive your message home in your speech.

Whatever you are trying to persuade the audience to do, it will take a significant effort to actually create change. You will need to back up your ideas, connect with the listeners, and gather their sympathies with touching examples and thoughtful presentation. This is a big job, requiring total commitment and heart for the task. You want your oratory to have the same impact that the ancient Greek orator Pericles attributed to his great rival Demosthenes. He said, "When Pericles speaks the people say, 'How well he speaks.' But when Demosthenes speaks the people say, 'Let us march!'" Commit to your message, express it in a convincing and simple thesis, and use the major techniques of persuasion to connect to the audience. Just like Demosthenes, you too can learn how to inspire an audience to march.

Expository Speaking

In real life, the type of public speech that you are most likely to be asked to give is a speech with the purpose of informing an audience about something. This is referred to as an expository speech, because it is intended to fully expose everything about a topic. The speech should enlighten the audience about its subject and is not necessarily intended to persuade them or cause them to take sides on an issue. To present information, the speaker may use visual aids. In competitive individual events, expository speaking is usually the only type of public speech that allows for the use of visual aids. Visual aids can include objects, pictures, charts, or anything else that you think will help the audience to gain further understanding of your topic.

Expository speaking teaches you how to explain complicated ideas and present information about a subject in an engaging manner. In the world, expository speaking is used by teachers, pastors, salesmen, news reporters, and many others. All of these speakers must explain the pertinent information about a topic of interest. No matter what you end up doing for the rest of your life, the time will come when you will be called on to give a presentation that describes something or present information about something. Whether this presentation is a class project in school, a Sunday School lesson at your church, or an earnings report for a company, you will need clarity, knowledge and documentation of your subject, and an enthusiastic presentation that holds the attention of the audience. There are a few simple rules for preparing a speech that helps the audience to grasp your ideas.

How it Works in Competition

Most leagues give you a ten minute time limit for expository speaking. In this form of public speaking, visual aids are allowed, and you should definitely use them. The overall goal of a good expository speech is to keep an audience entertained and fascinated by your presentation, to the point that they hardly realize how much information you are giving them. It is your responsibility to keep yourself energetic and interesting and think about creative ways to illustrate your topic. If you can learn how to do this well, you will definitely have a big step up when you have to do presentations for school and work. Your knowledge of expository speaking will give you the experience and skills that will make any public speaking situation a breeze.

Preparing an Expository Speech

Selecting a Topic: The best topics for expository speeches are subjects that interest you, such as your hobbies or your favorite things to learn about. You might want to give a speech about horse riding, baseball, or dolphins. If you are really interested in art, you could give a speech about the Mona Lisa. These can be good topics because you will already have a certain level of knowledge and enthusiasm about them, which will make it easier to prepare and deliver a speech.

Many speakers choose to give speeches about a lighthearted topic, an everyday object or item that most people take for granted. Recent expository speeches that have done well in competition have been about subjects like Spam, apples, and shoes. For example, in the speech about apples, the speaker talked about the history of apples and when they first became domesticated, some famous incidents in history that involved apples, nutritional information about apples, and some uncommon ways to use apples. The audience thought they knew something about apples before, but this speaker was able to open their eyes to a much broader understanding of them than they had imagined before.

Another common expository speech topic is new technologies or scientific knowledge, and the speaker may choose to notify the audience about some fascinating recent developments or the implications of new inventions. You can also choose to alert the audience to something they knew nothing about ahead of time, such as beekeeping or asbestos contamination in homes. Take an unusual or unexpected topic and explain it in detail. These speeches are especially good if you can take your unusual topic and explain how it affects the lives of your audience members in ways they might not have known about.

The important thing to keep in mind when choosing a topic is that it should interest the audience and you should be able to find plenty of information about it. You do not want to give a speech that has nothing new for the audience. The best expository speeches leave the audience saying, "Wow! I didn't know that!"

Preparation: When writing your speech, you want to do extensive research on the topic you have chosen. Go to the library and check out all the books you can find on your topic. Search the internet for information about it, and look in encyclopedias and other reference books to see what you can find. For some topics, you might even want to interview someone who is knowledgeable or make a field trip to gather ideas. If your speech is about apples, perhaps you could visit an orchard and talk to the farmer.

It can be difficult to write a good outline for an expository speech. Too many expository speeches sound like nothing more than a jumble of facts that

"May my teaching drop like the rain, my speech condense like the dew; like gentle rain on grass, like showers on new growth."
- Deuteronomy 32:2

57

have no connection except that they are all about the same subject. Your speech will be improved if you can organize your facts into a few main areas. For example, you may choose to write about the history of your subject, the different ways in which it is used today, and some surprising or little-known details about it. The organization requirements may be less rigid than they are with other types of speeches, but you should organize your material and avoid jumping around randomly.

Facts are easily forgotten. In your expository speech, you will be presenting a large variety of facts, and you probably do not want the audience to forget them. This means that you want to think about how to connect the information you are sharing with the audience. Visual aids can be very helpful with this task, because an audience will remember something much better if they can read it or look at it while they hear it.

In addition to this, you want to use images and language that will help to give the audience a picture of what you are talking about. If you describe the size of something, compare it to an object that the audience is familiar with. If you are giving a date that something happened, list one or two other things that were going on at the same time. Whatever you are presenting, you want to make sure that it is clear and memorable for the audience.

Visual Aids: Good visual aids are the cornerstone of a solid expository speech. You can use visual aids to get attention, to clarify a point, or to convey information. The most common visual aids are two-dimensional, such as pictures, charts, and graphs. Because of this, most expository speakers display their visual aids on board, using an easel. If you want to incorporate more creative visual aids, you can use three-dimensional objects as well. A speech on jazz might be spiced up if you show off your saxophone, and a speech about the circus could be helped by some juggling. You might want to bring examples of the object you are talking about or do a demonstration of an activity, complete with props. This might mean taking a box or a bag of props with you into your round.

In most speech leagues, there are almost no rules for the type of visual aids that you can use in an expository speech. The main restriction is that everything you use must be set up and taken down within the ten minute time limit, and your time begins when your name is called, not when you begin speaking. If you just have an easel and a box, this is not a problem. When your name is called, simply carry them to the front of the room and begin. The only real limit is on overly extravagant or elaborate visual aids that require lengthy setup or cleanup. For example, if you were to toss confetti during your speech, you would have to sweep up every last bit of confetti before your time was up, which means that confetti might be a bad idea. The focus should be on how you use visuals in your speech, not on how much stuff you can put together in ten minutes.

When planning your visual aids, keep in mind that every visual should have a clear purpose that is connected to your speech. You do not want the audience to wonder what is the point of the picture that you are displaying. You should space your visuals evenly throughout your speech, with aids to help you with each new point you make or fact you present. Do not go through several visuals at the beginning and then have a long stretch without them. Also, make sure that you have a wide variety of visual aids to keep the audience interested. It is easy to make a bunch of boards each with a single picture and a brief caption, but the audience will get bored from so many of the same boards.

You want to plan for visuals that help you to clarify and enhance the message of your speech, not confuse or clutter it. Think about whether you want a lot of visuals that you can go through quickly or a few visuals that have been carefully selected for their impact. Many visuals work well with a humorous or lighthearted speech, especially when you have sight gags and cartoon-style pictures. A few visuals that are more serious work well for a more thoughtful speech.

To make your visual aids, rely on sturdy, high-quality materials. You will be speaking many times over the course of a competitive season and you do not want your visuals to fall apart. You can buy durable, thick posterboards or foam-core boards at a good office supply or craft store. Keep the visuals neat and simple for a crisp and professional appearance. Be careful when attaching pictures and text, and make sure it looks clean and nice. The audience should be able to focus on what you want the visual to convey, not on the sloppy job you did when you were making it.

"Things seen are mightier than things heard."
- Alfred, Lord Tennyson

The key to a memorable speech is to be creative with your visuals. You can add extra touches by using Velcro. For example, an expository speech about Russian culture featured a visual aid that gave facts about the people of Russia. The visual was a board with a picture of one of those Russian nesting dolls on it. The picture had a fact about Russia on it and it was Velcroed to the board. When the speaker pulled it off, it revealed a smaller nesting doll with another fact, and so on. This was a more interesting way of presenting this information than simply giving a list of the facts.

You can also make visuals with hidden doors, transparent overlays, and pull out flaps. Look at children's books for inspiration and ideas. Your visuals should be clear and eye-catching, and illustrate what you are saying in your speech. Avoid having too much small text or overly complicated imagery, both of which will encourage the audience to spend more time trying to figure out your visuals aids than listening to you.

Avoid relying solely on two-dimensional visuals. You can use actual objects such as a soccer ball, a toy train or a chocolate bar to provide variety. Some speakers also enjoy adding some articles of clothing, such as wearing one of those helmets with a light on it in a speech about cave exploration. A highlight of a recent speech on duct tape was the speaker showing off his duct tape necktie.

During your speech, make sure that you are in control of your visuals. Make sure that they are easy to transport and that they require little setup. Always practice your speech as much as possible to make sure that you can handle your visuals well. If there is a part in your speech where you are not referring to any visual aids for a while, it is a good idea to hide them away from view with a blank board so that the audience will pay attention to you.

If your visuals have text on them, you should read them aloud as part of your speech when you first display them. This is to keep yourself and the audience on the same page, and to prevent them from reading your visuals while you are talking about something else. It is also helpful to arrange your visuals from back to front. It is easier to pull the next visual out from the back and place it in front than it is to shove a picture behind the others when you are done with it. If you have extra objects, hide them in a box or bag. If possible, put this box on a desk or hang it from the easel so you do not have to stoop down to the floor to pick things up during your speech.

To keep your visual aids in good condition, purchase a case to keep them in. Check over them before every tournament to make sure they are in good shape and the Velcro or glue is still sticking. If they are starting to look worn, consider replacing or fixing them. You might need to replace a picture or trim the edges of your boards. Never go to a tournament with shabby or sloppy visual aids.

There is always a chance that something will go wrong during your speech. I recently saw an expository speech in which the easel collapsed, scattering the visual aids all over the floor. Rather than panic, the speaker smiled, cracked a few jokes while gathering everything up and putting it back together, and then continued without missing a step. If you maintain your composure, you will win over the audience no matter what happens to you.

Conclusion: An expository speech should provide a complete picture of the topic you are describing. You want to present information in a clear, enjoyable manner and strive to educate the audience about your subject. Judges are instructed to consider the overall effectiveness of your presentation as well as the quality of information, and whether or not you are telling them anything that they did not already know. Make sure you do the in-depth research that is necessary to have fascinating facts about your subject, and also work on striking visual aids and an enthusiastic delivery. As you learn how to explain anything to any audience, expository speaking will teach you how to integrate both style and substance.

Extemporaneous Speaking

Extemporaneous speaking, which is called extemp by speech competitors, is simply the most valuable and rewarding competitive speech event, bar none. Through participating in extemp you will be developing life skills that are fundamentally important but are available nowhere else in school. You will be researching and formulating opinions about issues and problems of which most teenagers are completely unaware. You will learn how to quickly analyze a complicated and difficult question and explain it in terms that can be understood by anyone. The tools you pick up through extemporaneous speaking will help you in every other area of your life.

Extemporaneous speaking turns everyone who does it into a great researcher. With its emphasis on current events, extemp will make you keep up on the important news of the day and create research files on what is happening all around the world. Before you ever go to a tournament you will find the research you do for extemp broadening your perspective and giving you a new understanding and appreciation of politics, economics, and other important issues. As you become a more informed, knowledgeable individual you will learn how to gather information and organize it effectively, a skill that will be essential to your continued education. Students who have participated in extemp are able to do re-

"Extemporaneous speaking should be practiced and cultivated."
- Abraham Lincoln

search projects and write papers much more quickly than others.

Above and beyond simple fact-gathering, extemporaneous speaking will enable you to think through your own opinions of these issues and critically examine what you believe. Not only will you have to come to your own conclusions but you will also learn how to deliver them in a way that will be appreciated by your audience. In extemp you do not have the chance to carefully craft each word and phrase in a pre-scripted presentation. You must maintain a sense of purpose and organization without hiding behind the protection of a manuscript, as you learn to present your ideas with conviction, wit, and aplomb. This ability is crucial to leadership and it is no wonder that the top ranks of business, media, and politics are dotted with former extemporaneous speakers.

When the American Founding Fathers and European Enlightenment thinkers laid the groundwork for our modern democracy, they knew that it would only work if the people remained intelligent and thoughtful about broad social and cultural issues. To our detriment we have lost that vision and far too many modern American citizens are unable to analyze and articulate a reasoned response to the problems and controversies that constantly arise in the real world. Open and informed discussion is the life blood of a free society. To maintain the strength and vitality of our society we need people who are able to examine complex problems in the light of evidence and logic and discuss important questions without resorting to personal attacks or broad generalizations. Extemporaneous speaking is an invaluable tool toward that end.

Extemporaneous speakers are informed and thoughtful citizens with a solid perspective on the shape of world affairs. They are confident and capable communicators, able to speak fluently and with authority even in the absence of notes or extensive preparation. They understand how to use a number of sources to analyze an issue and boil it down to its most important points and then explain those points with clarity. They have learned the skills that will serve them well in school, in their jobs, and in leadership positions throughout society.

How it Works in Competition

Extemporaneous speaking is the most difficult and challenging of the individual events and requires the most work. To be a successful extemporaneous speaker you must stay informed on what is going on in the world and work with the other extempers in your club or school to prepare extensive research files on current events. When you arrive at a competition you will be sent to the extemp prep room. At the appropriate time you will be called forward to draw three topics on a piece of paper. The topics are always in the form of a question about current events and you can choose any one of them.

On selecting your topic you will go to the research files which you brought and grab all the relevant information that you can find. Using this research you have thirty minutes to prepare a speech addressing the topic. At the end of thirty minutes you will be asked to deliver a seven minute speech. In most tournaments, the speaker is allowed to use a note card during the speech.

Preparing for Extemporaneous Speaking

Research:
Extemp is a multifaceted event. No matter how talented you are as a speaker, it is impossible to do well in extemp by just showing up at a tournament and winging it. You will be constantly working on research, keeping up on headlines and big news stories. The first and most important characteristic of a successful extemporaneous speaker is research.

Sources: Extemp research begins with the big three news magazines; *Time*, *Newsweek*, and *U.S. News and World Report*. These will become your best friends, as they provide a clear and readable overview of both domestic and international affairs. Some speech leagues use only topics that have been covered in one of these magazines. Christian students will also be helped by *World* magazine which covers the same issues from a distinctly Biblical viewpoint. Another important resource is *The Economist*, the magazine that gives the best weekly overview of news around the world. All of these magazines offer a great starting place for both information and analysis of the most important current events.

News magazines offer an excellent beginning, but you will want to do research that is much more focused and in depth in order to be competitive. Newspapers are an important source for reporting and commentary and usually provide a more detailed and balanced perspective. They are also able to cover many more stories than magazines have space for. While it is acceptable to use your local paper, it is better if you have access to the big national newspapers. Extemp favorites include *The New York Times*, *The Wall Street Journal*, *USA Today*, *The Washington Post*, and *The Christian Science Monitor*. You can generally access any major newspaper either on the internet or at your local library. Because extemp topics are always very current, you want to focus on newspaper articles from the past month or so.

If you can get connected to a good electronic database, you will be able to do your research much more effectively and comprehensively. The most popular of these is *Lexis/Nexis*, which you can probably find at the library of a local college or university. These libraries will usually let you in to use their databases and computers, so you should definitely utilize them. *Lexis/Nexis*, along with *Westlaw*, its major competitor, has archives of many newspapers, legal journals, and other publications from around the world. I also really enjoy *ProQuest*, a service that you should be able to find at many public library systems. *ProQuest* offers a selection of national newspapers and magazines.

"Were it left to me to decide whether we should have a government without newspapers or newspapers without a government, I should not hesitate a moment to prefer the latter."
- *Thomas Jefferson*

The internet is a great source for a wide variety of information, with the distinct advantage of being much faster and cheaper than conventional sources. The best extempers find great firsthand perspectives from Asian and European newspapers and other international sources, many of which have their own websites. Using the internet comes with a huge caveat, however. It is full of all sorts of wild and crazy people spinning their own tales and half-truths. Make sure that you use only research from credible sources. A good rule of thumb is that you should only cite sources in your speeches that most audiences will either know about or be able to gauge the credibility of. The *British Broadcasting Corporation* website is great, but stay away from those junior high students who have their own personal web pages.

Extemp Files: At this point you are probably wondering what exactly you are going to do with all this research, anyway. The answer is that you are going to be developing what is known as an extemp file. The first rule of extemp files is that it is much easier to make them a team effort. Get all the extempers in your speech club or school together, and practice division of labor. Everyone should concentrate on researching a few specific topics. Collect several articles on each "hot spot," the major issues that are receiving substantial coverage in the news. Remember that any of these could surface as an extemp topic, and it is best to be prepared.

You can also enlist your parents and siblings to help research. Younger brothers and sisters do a great job of looking through newspapers and magazines and clipping news stories about specific subjects such as the Middle East. If your parents already read and watch the news daily, you can ask them to help you keep informed on the most important stories.

It is impossible to predict what the most popular topics will be in any given year. Your best guide will be to know what events are getting the most coverage in the big media outlets. Extemp topics are generally split between domestic and international issues, so know what sort of questions to expect in your league. Domestic topics usually center around things like political developments, economic issues, and social concerns like crime, education, and immigration. International topics are usually concentrated in areas where there are crises or conflicts going on. You should have a good idea of the big happenings in both America and the world, and be prepared with evidence for anything.

An extemp file is usually a big box filled with clearly labeled file folders, each of which contains articles on a specific subject. For example, you will have a file folder labeled "Social Security," one labeled "Foreign Policy With China," and so on. Definitely avoid the rookie mistake of just throwing a bunch of magazines into a box and trying to keep an index of what is in each one. That is what I did my first few tournaments, and I ended up spending more than half of my prep time flipping through magazines looking for articles. You need to clip out articles and separate them into file folders. Arrange the folders alphabetically in your box, and your time at the tournament will be simple. When you draw your topic, all you have to do is pull out the folder that has articles on that subject.

As you work with your team members on preparing a file, always be sure that you have research on any topic you could encounter. Organize your labor so everything is covered. Also, while it is great to split the work up with other extempers, this does not give you an excuse to concentrate on your assignments only. You need to keep your knowledge up on all subjects and have a basic grasp of the main issues in every major news story. By staying well-read, you will be much better equipped to deal with the specific topic which you draw. Keep in mind that the better grasp you have of your topic, the more persuasive and professional will be the speech that you give.

Topics: Extemp topics are always in the form of a question, and usually very specific in their intent. You will rarely see a topic like "Explain what is going on in Iraq." A far more likely topic would be along the lines of "Will weapons inspectors be allowed back into Iraq?" The topic will require you to take the general knowledge and information you have about a subject, and use it to examine one aspect of the issue. There are three possible types of questions that you will be asked to address. They are questions of fact, questions of value, and questions of policy.

Most of the questions that you encounter in extemp will be simple questions of fact. They are asking you to analyze an event or issue, and make a reasonable explanation of what happened or a prediction of what will happen. It is important that you stick to the question, and don't try to answer a different question. If the question is "Who will win the Republican Presidential nomination?" it will not do you any good to tell who you think should win the nomination. If you have a topic asking you how you think the Supreme Court will rule on an upcoming case, you should examine the question from the perspective of things like the legal precedents in the case and how the Court members seem to be leaning, but you should not go off on a long rant about why society will collapse if the Court does not rule the way you think it should. Maybe you are right, but you are not answering the question.

Questions of value are more rare than questions of fact. In fact, it is often a big mistake to interpret questions of fact as questions of value. Topics such as "How have American attitudes toward business changed in the wake of recent corporate misdeeds?" or "What are the social and cultural implications of new developments in human cloning?" may seem highly value-oriented, but a careful examination reveals that neither of these actually requires a value judgment. People with different perspectives can still agree on how American attitudes are changing, whether they like it or not. Even when you draw a controversial, value-oriented topic, try to remain objective, and take into account both sides of the discussion in your speech. Remember that you don't know what your audience thinks about the subject, and it is never a good idea in any speaking situation to make inflammatory statements or controversial assumptions. Speak your mind, but be sensitive and careful in doing so.

The final type of question is the question of policy, which are rather common to extemporaneous speaking. You will often be asked to describe some sort of policy solution to a problem, in topics such as "How should Congress resolve the Social Security crisis?" or "What changes should be made to the campaign finance system?" In these instances, you will need to analyze the problem and provide a workable solution, usually something that is being proposed already either by Congress or by experts in the field. Policy questions are generally less controversial than value topics, but when issues such as capital punishment and gun control are presented, bear in mind that your audience probably already has a strong opinion one way or the other. You should always attempt to consider all viewpoints as you explain why you believe one proposal is the best.

It is never a good idea to pick a topic about which you have no knowledge and no articles in your extemp file. In one round that I judged, one of the speakers argued that his topic couldn't possibly be a big problem because he couldn't find any articles in his file about it. This may have been creative, but it made him look poorly prepared and not serious about the issues. It is always a better idea to choose a topic that you know you can respond to intelligently using your research.

Using Preparation Time: After selecting your topic, you should go back to your extemp file and pull out the appropriate folder. If you and your teammates have done your job, it will be brimming with articles and information on the subject. You now face the task of turning all of this into an intelligible presentation in the course of thirty minutes. This is where many first-timers break down, but in reality the task is not that difficult after you have learned the basic method for preparing an extemporaneous speech.

The very first thing, and the most important thing to make your speech worthwhile, is to answer the question. Take the topic you draw and carefully think it over. Ask yourself what kind of question it is and what sort of answer it requires. Make absolutely sure that you do not misunderstand its vocabulary, grammar, or context. You should write your answer to the question right up at the top of your note card and use it as the thesis around which you will construct your entire speech. The biggest mistake made by extempers of all experience levels is failing to answer the question directly and clearly. Your audience will know what your topic is, and judges are instructed to listen for how well you respond to your specific question.

When you give your speech you should state the answer to the question explicitly right near the beginning. Don't try to cloud the issue, dodge it, or straddle the fence to avoid the controversy. Any intelligent audience member can sense obfuscation instantly. This does mean that you could be taking positions the judge will disagree with, but as long as you present your point of view thoughtfully and back it up, judges will respect you more for that than for double talk.

Once you have formulated the answer to your question, you should begin to write the outline for your speech. To do this, follow all of the major rules of speechwriting which have already been discussed. Of course, you will not have time to write and memorize a manuscript, so you will only get through the outline stage. There are a few special considerations for writing an extemp outline.

It is impossible to overestimate the importance of the introduction in extemporaneous speaking. You absolutely must have a good, solid attention getter to connect with the audience and make your speech stand out from the other five or six in the round. Review the section on introductions in the speechwriting section and think about examples of different types of introductions you could use.

The best extempers have a number of introductions which they know they will be able to plug into virtually any topic. For example, one of my favorite introductions when competing in extemp revolved around the true story of how I once got caught cheating at a game when I was a little boy, and how I learned the absolute importance of playing by the rules. I used it to lead into any topic about a problem resulting from corruption, lies, or attempts to beat the system. I could use this story to give a speech about Brazil's economic problems, campaign finance scandals, and Social Security, in addition to a number of other widely diverse topics. The introduction worked because it communicated a simple and universal truth in a way that allowed me to personally connect with the audience, and also because it was a familiar, homey analogy that could be applied to a number of serious real-world topics.

Personal stories can be great sources for introductions, but you can also use events in history, or even completely fictional scenarios that you can use to illustrate the central issue in your topic. Many extempers use sports analogies, or examples from nature that will help the audience to grasp a concept which is important to their thesis. Be careful with prepared introductions, however. Do not make the common mistake of trying to force an introduction onto your speech just because it has worked for you in the past. Always find an introduction that fits the topic, not the other way around. Your speech must function as a cohesive whole, with all the parts working together to add to your message. Even if you use a certain introduction for many speeches, the audience should always think that you created it with this specific speech in mind.

After planning your introduction you should concentrate on the body of your speech. Construct a three point outline that provides a complete answer to your question. There are many ways to organize your speech, but you should always adapt it to the information that you have about the topic.

First, decide how much background information the audience will need. Most people will have no prior knowledge whatsoever about many topics, particularly those about other parts of the world, and thus you will need to give them a good explanation of what has lead up to the current state of affairs. For other topics, particularly those that have been discussed and analyzed from all possible angles by the media, it would be foolish and redundant to spend much time explaining the nature of the issue.

Next, consider how much of the information in your files can be used in your speech. As a general rule, use as much actual evidence as you can from as many sources as possible. The best extemporaneous speakers are able to back up every major point they make with a solid piece of evidence. If you have done a good job on research, then you should be able to present a rich variety of source material for your speech. If your topic is about the President's trip to India, for example, your speech will be much more informative and memorable if you use an article from an Indian publication along with the standard American sources.

Based on the articles you have about your topic, write down your main arguments in support of how you answered the question. As in any speech, it is best to organize your outline in line with some overarching structure. You could examine three possible solutions to a problem, explain a problem and then provide a solution, or discuss the pros and cons of a certain topic or issue. Many extemporaneous speeches can best be arranged chronologically, in which case the speaker looks at the past, present, and future of an issue, or regionally, which is when the speaker examines the effects of a problem in several different geographic areas. These are just a few of the many possible outline structures used by

Sidebar: Extemp Outline Structure

When preparing an extemporaneous speech, your outline should end up looking like this:

I. Introduction
    A. Hook
    B. Thesis – Answer the question!
    C. Preview main pts.
- transition to …

II. Point A
    A. Evidence/ Illustration
    B. Application to Thesis
- transition to …

III. Point B
    A. Evidence/ Illustration
    B. Application to Thesis
- transition to …

IV. Point C
    A. Evidence/ Illustration
    B. Application to Thesis
- transition to …

V. Conclusion
    A. Review main pts.
    B. Justify thesis – Answer the question!
    C. End on a strong note – refer back to intro hook

Notice how the structure of the speech is symmetrical. The introduction and conclusion mirror each other to give the speech a feeling of completeness.

successful extempers, and you should always be able to come up with one that fits your specific topic.

The conclusion of an extemp speech needs to fulfill three basic functions. It should restate the major points of the speech, leave no doubt as to the answer to the question, and tie everything back to the introduction. You should have a basic idea of what you will say in your conclusion, and go ahead and write it down on your note paper.

To sum up, in preparation time you should write down a clear and concise answer to the topic question. You should then plot out the outline to your speech around that answer, organizing your major points, an introduction, and a conclusion. All of the points should have one or more citations to back them up, and the whole speech should flow together as a whole. Although most leagues do not allow you to use notes during your speech, you should always write down your outline. You will not remember it, or any of your sources, if you have not written them down and visually stored them in your brain.

All of this may sound like a lot to do in thirty minutes, but actually you should only use about twenty to twenty-three minutes in writing your speech. Always leave the last seven to ten minutes to practice delivering it. You will not be able to deliver your very best speech if you do not run through it before the actual performance. Go right up to a wall and speak your heart out. This will help you get a better feel for how the speech will flow, as well as identifying those points and citations that you are having trouble remembering. Review these quickly before you go to deliver the speech for real.

Delivery: For the most part, extemp delivery should be like any platform speech. Eye contact should be direct and consistent, gestures should be planned to heighten interest and meaning, and your voice should be loud and confident. You should be in complete control of your body and move several times over the course of the speech to mark transitions between points. Refer back to the speechwriting portion of this book for further general delivery tips.

There are certain extemp pitfalls to watch out for, however. The first of these is the general tendency to say "um" and "uh" and other verbalizations that distract from your message, or to trip over words and phrases. This always happened to me when giving a speech about Chinese or Russian political leaders. Names like Primakov and Xiaoping do not exactly roll off the tongue. This is very difficult to avoid when you are not allowed to use a manuscript, but it is of great importance. Speaking fluently will markedly improve your showing in extemporaneous competition. It makes you sound infinitely more confident, believable, and as if you have actually thought through what you are going to say. In fact, one of the great benefits of extemp is that it will make you into a much more fluent speaker.

While it is easy to give lip service to speaking without saying "um" and "uh," it is phenomenally difficult to actually accomplish this. Although you can improve with practice, many speakers find that these are so unconscious that they are almost impossible to get rid of. As you practice your speaking, listen for it and make a conscious effort to eliminate it. One speaker I knew would say "um" constantly, ten or fifteen times a minute. Finally, her coach simply yelled "UM" at her every time she said it, and she quickly rid herself of the habit. Subsequently, she became one of the most fluent, confident, and effective speakers I have ever heard.

A second habit many competitors in extemp fall into is that they begin to speak at increasingly rapid rates. Almost unanimously, judges want you to slow down, and greatly appreciate it when they can actually follow your speech. It is better to say something precisely and slowly with a few well-chosen words than in a roundabout way with so many words that you have to talk at light speed to fit them all in. A great extemporaneous speaker should cover all the

"In oratory the greatest art is to hide art."
- Jonathan Swift

necessary points at a rate that is easy on the ears and brains of the audience.

Of course, you will make mistakes and verbal slip-ups, and not even the best speaker is perfect. When you do mispronounce a name, never allow yourself to get flustered or frustrated. Simply smile, correct yourself, and keep on going. The more you practice extemp, the more dynamic you will become as a speaker, and the more you will amaze yourself and your audiences with a delivery that sounds as if you had practiced each speech for months.

Ideas for Improving

Overnight Extemp: When you are just getting started in extemp, the thirty minute time period can be very intimidating. For your first few practice speeches, have your coach or one of your team mates give you a topic a day in advance. Spend some time carefully preparing the speech, learning how to write and remember an outline. Become comfortable with going through a whole stack of articles on a subject and finding the few nuggets of information that you need for your specific topic. Practice the speech two or three times before you actually give it, developing your ability to allocate your time appropriately and tie your introduction, body, and conclusion together for maximum effect. As you gain experience, begin to cut down on your preparation time while keeping the quality of your speeches high, until you can prepare and deliver an excellent speech within just thirty minutes every time.

Throwing Darts: This activity will improve your dart-throwing abilities just as much as your extemp skills, but it can be a fun way for you to practice. Either use a map of the world for international extemp, or a list of topics for United States extemp. Throw darts at the map or list, and see how much information you can provide about the topic you hit. If you do not like the idea of darts, then put topics in a jar and draw them, or come up with any way of selecting topics randomly. The goal is to identify the weak points in your research and knowledge, and also to practice using your extemp file to respond to a specific question.

Team Meetings: Extemp is definitely easier when you have several people in your club or school working together. You should meet regularly with your fellow extempers, and assign each other different areas of the news to research. When you get together, everyone should explain what they have been researching, providing the most important names, places, and developments. Even though everyone is specializing in certain areas, all of you should stay aware of as much as you can. Seek out opportunities to test yourself in your knowledge of what is going on. One way I did this was to take the news quizzes that my local newspaper published every week. Have your coach, parent, or teammate throw out a name or set of initials and try to name who that person is or what organization those initials stand for, as well as what major current events they play a role in.

Final Thoughts

Extemporaneous speaking can seem overwhelming to the beginner. It seems inconceivable to be able to pull together such a massive amount of research and be prepared to give a fluent, well supported speech on almost any topic imaginable. Do not give up if it seems hopeless. It is acceptable and expected that you will start small and gradually build up your research files as you go along. No one can be perfect in extemporaneous speaking from the beginning, and if you could, there would be no reason to practice it. If you wait to start getting involved until you think you are ready, you will never get involved. Extemporaneous speaking offers tremendous learning benefits that can not be earned from the sidelines. The best advice I can give you is to realize that it is a learning process, get involved to the best of your ability, and improve as you go along. You will surprise yourself at how much you can accomplish if you never limit yourself.

Impromptu Speaking

Impromptu speaking is at once the easiest and most difficult of the individual events. It is easy in that no writing, memorization, or extensive research on a topic is required. It is difficult in that no writing, memorization, or extensive research on a topic is allowed. The dictionary defines an "impromptu" speech as one which is "performed or conceived without rehearsal or preparation," or simply "spontaneous." Due to the lack of any chance to prepare, you may be frightened by impromptu, or think you couldn't possibly prepare such a long speech on such short notice. Other students fall into the opposite trap, believing that they have finally found an event which requires no work, and they can succeed just by showing up at a tournament and ad libbing. In reality, impromptu does require extensive work but utilizes a unique set of skills that can and should be mastered by everyone.

Many people think they would never be able to do something like impromptu because it seems so imposing. This perception is rooted in the myth that impromptu requires you to think quickly. Actually, everybody already has the ability to think quickly, whether you realize it or not, and what impromptu does is teach you how to organize your thoughts. If you have any special interests or hobbies that you really enjoy, any books or songs that have significant meaning for you, or anything else that makes you the unique individual you are, then you have the potential to be a great impromptu speaker. This event

"It usually takes more than three weeks to prepare a good impromptu speech."
- Mark Twain

will help you learn how to weave these life experiences into an arresting presentation and how to use your very own interests and opinions to relate abstract concepts to real life, and to do all of this on the spot and under pressure as well. This skill is invaluable, and it can help you to be an interesting, witty, and confident person. Impromptu speaking is a perfect workshop for developing these valuable personal qualities, and you will take its lessons with you through classrooms, meetings, job interviews, and involvement in your community.

How it Works in Competition

An impromptu competition is a fairly simple event. Speakers enter the room one by one and draw three topics on slips of paper from an envelope. The topics will be either quotations or abstractions. A quotation is simply a statement about life, usually uttered by someone famous. It should express some general outlook or philosophy to which the speaker can respond. These are generally of the "Give me liberty or give me death" or "Life is like a box of chocolates" variety. An abstraction is one word, almost always an intangible one. Topics in this category can include values, emotions, or concepts, words like "envy," "mystery," and "truth."

As soon as the speaker draws three topics, preparation time begins. The speaker has two minutes to prepare a speech on any one of these three topics. After two minutes, the speaker is given five minutes to deliver his or her speech, using no notes. The speech should present an opinion about the topic and defend that opinion with a clear logical outline. An impromptu speaker is expected to draw from a wide variety of knowledge and experience to support his or her opinion, using evidence, illustrations, and examples which are appropriate and contribute to the overall effectiveness of the presentation. The speech is judged on content, delivery, and organization.

Impromptu can be one of the most entertaining individual events to watch. A great impromptu speech takes a seemingly abstract or theoretical topic and applies it to real life, giving the audience something instructive and provocative to think about and act on. To do this, you will need to engage every part of your brain. Your speech should be creative and entertaining enough to keep the audience's attention, but you also must have solid content and organization so your speech has a real impact. This can only be accomplished when you find your own personality, and learn how to express your won thoughts and ideas in a way that fits your style.

Solid content

How to Deliver an Impromptu Speech

I remember how I felt when I had to deliver my first impromptu speech:
The room wasn't cold, but it felt that way. The unblinking eyes of the audience bored holes into my brain, puncturing my concentration and letting any confidence and coherency drain away. I desperately tried to bring the small slip of paper into focus, but it danced around in my trembling hands, evading my frantic thoughts. I squirmed in my seat like a seven year old in a church service, punctuating my agony by inventing increasingly creative and noisy ways to clear my throat. When the time came, my speech was an intense battle against any semblance of meaning or thoughtfulness, and all observers agreed that meaning and thoughtfulness lost without putting up much of an effort.

If this sounds anything like your first experience with impromptu, then you are not alone. The new experience of encountering a completely unexpected topic, and being required to deliver an interesting and uplifting presentation on this topic almost immediately, can be disorienting. However, I cannot stress enough that everyone possesses the ability to do this well. There are certain mental tools that help you unleash your brain power, plus a simple five step method that is a prerequisite for a great impromptu speech.

Step 1: Decide on a thesis. The first thing to do upon selecting your topic is to formulate a thesis. Decide what the point of your speech is going to be. If the topic is a quotation, the easiest thesis is to either agree or disagree with the statement. If it is an abstraction, try to figure out how to apply the concept to current issues or real life. In one sentence, say something true about this concept or principle. It is important to develop a solid thesis before you begin formulating your speech. The thesis gives your thoughts direction, and provides your speech with a purpose.

A good thesis should be specific, easy to understand, and meaningful enough to hang your speech around. Think about some aspect of the topic you have drawn that connects to a good message you can share with an audience. If you draw the abstract topic "church," do not just try to pull together a speech about church. Instead, formulate a crisp thesis, such as "Each member of the church has an important role in God's plan for the world." It is much better to give a speech supporting this thesis than just to talk about the word "church" for five minutes.

Step 2: Think of some illustrations to support your thesis. Now that you have a thesis, begin thinking about how to support it and how to provide evidence for what you are trying to say. This is where your personality enters the picture in a big way. You are trying to prove a simple proposition about a topic, and to do this you will need to give some examples of its truth. The place to find these examples is in your own life. Has anything happened to you that illustrates the truth of the thesis? Do any aspects of your favorite activities support your point? If your thesis is about the value of hard work, then talk about an achievement of which you are proud. If you are talking about the importance of caring for others, give an illustration about something kind you did for someone, or, better yet, something kind that someone else did for you. You should be able to come up with a personal example for just about any thesis you want to support.

Personal examples are only one option, however. Try thinking about famous persons in history or characters from your favorite books and movies. Surely you can think of some individual or story that will help you support your point. Incorporate current events or fairy tales and children's literature. Remember that anything can be used in an impromptu speech. Your speech will be much more interesting if you can communicate some special knowledge you have. If you love science, play an instrument, or have a pet, you have material to talk about.

You want to have a variety of examples and illustrations to support your ideas. When you are just getting started, you will probably only be able to come up with one story in two minutes. As you gain experience, however, you will become better at pulling out interesting examples from your own knowledge. By practicing impromptu speaking, you will learn what makes for a good story and how to pull one together quickly.

Step 3: Develop an Introduction. Use a story, joke, fact, or quotation that you think will grab your audience's attention at the beginning. Speakers call this a hook. It is very important to have something to grab the audience right from the start, instead of simply reading your topic to them. This book discusses the role of a speech introduction in depth in the chapter on speechwriting, so you should refer back to that for more information.

Because of the limited amount of time you have to prepare, it is probably best to use one of the examples that you came up with in Step 2 as your introduction. Many good impromptu speakers begin by introducing a story that connects to their topic, and leaving the audience in suspense about how the story ends until the conclusion of their speech. This can help you to make your speech seem complete

Sidebar: Top Ten Sources for Stories

It can be difficult to quickly think of examples and illustrations to use in an impromptu speech. These are some good places to begin when scanning your memory for stories.

1. Hobbies. Take examples from your pastimes and things you enjoy.

2. Family. Tell a story about yourself. Personal stories are the best!

3. The Bible. Use Bible stories and principles to support your thesis.

4. History. Use the past to illustrate the present.

5. Literature. Tell stories from books you have read.

6. Movies. Characters in movies can also illustrate an idea or concept.

7. Current Events. Use illustrations pulled from the headlines.

8. Nature. Find stories in the animal kingdom.

9. Fairy Tales. These have good morals.

10. Sports Analogies can be helpful as well.

and well-prepared even though you came up with it in a hurry.

Remember that an introduction is more than just a hook. You also want to make sure that you state the topic you have drawn, present your thesis, and preview the main points you will be using to support your thesis. Never leave any doubt about what message you intend to communicate in your speech.

Step 4: Plan Your Outline. A good outline has several main points that support your thesis. This structure is also covered in the chapter on speechwriting. All of the same rules apply to impromptu speaking as to any other speech that you write, with the only difference being the time constraints that you have when delivering an impromptu speech.

Because of these time constraints, it can be helpful to organize your speech around a common organizational structure. For example, you could talk about your topic in the past, the present, and the future. Another simple tool for organization is to lay out a problem, present a solution to the problem, and then give some of the benefits of your proposed solution. Many impromptu topics are best illustrated by beginning with some Biblical principles in support of your thesis, presenting a historical or personal example of the importance of the thesis, and then applying this message to the world today.

All of these outline structures assist you to organize your thoughts clearly and efficiently, and they also help the audience to follow what you are saying. Remember to make it very clear what your main points are. Do not just say, "Today I have three examples of this." Say something like, "In this speech I will be examining this topic from three different points of view; a personal perspective, a historical perspective, and a literary perspective," or "Let's take a look at how this concept affects the worlds of science, of religion, and of art." Your speech should be enjoyable and easy to listen to.

Step 5: Think About Your Transitions and Conclusions. Your final step, the thing you should be thinking about as you walk to the front of the room to begin talking, is polishing your presentation with smooth transitions and a good conclusion. You do not want your speech to sound choppy, like you are struggling through an outline that you have just come up with. Instead you want to appear professional and in control of your thoughts and your words.

Make sure that you provide a logical connection from your introduction to your thesis, from your thesis to your main points, and between each main point in your speech. These transitions make you much easier to listen to.

You also want to think about how to wrap everything up at the end. An effective conclusion should restate your major points and firmly entrench your thesis in the minds of the listeners. Once you have your outline, with an introduction leading into a thesis, three main points backed by examples, and a conclusion which summarizes the message for the audience members, you are ready to go.

You probably won't be able to incorporate all of these suggestions in your first attempt. In fact, at the beginning, you may think there is no way that you will ever be able to put together all the parts of a successful impromptu in just two minutes. Keep working at it. Nobody is able to perform perfectly from the start, and it takes significant practice before you feel comfortable with it. As you gain experience, you will become better and better at drawing together a wide variety of ideas to bring into your speech. You will begin to develop your own style as you figure out what works for you and what doesn't. Before long, you will love the challenge impromptu provides, and will discover what a thrill it is to create a well-delivered impromptu.

Ideas for Improving

The most straightforward approach to improving your impromptu skills is to practice the actual event. Have someone give you three topics and two minutes to prepare. If you are having trouble with this, and showing no improvement, then one of the following two activities could be helpful.

The Coloring Game: This is an excellent drill to try by yourself or with a group. It really helps you begin to think the way impromptu requires. Pick a color, and begin talking about it. Ask a few simple questions. Where do you observe this color in nature? What are some popular phrases that refer to this color? What values, ideas, or concepts does this color symbolize? Try to find a common thread that ties these things together. For example, the color green instantly brings to mind a number of specific images. We think of green lights which mean "go," plants and growth, money and greed, and the phrase "green with envy," among other things. Upon further thought, these concepts all fit a common pattern. Each one involves growth, production, the quest and desire for more, and a pattern of ever-increasing expansion. See if you can spin this common thread into the theme of a speech on the color green, complete with a thesis, outline, introduction, and the other parts of a well constructed speech. Then try other colors. What do we associate with red, blue, yellow, purple, white, black, etc.? Try this drill *ad infinitum* or *ad nauseam*, whichever comes first. If you can deliver a speech on a color, you can deliver a speech about anything.

Storytime: This drill will help you to practice incorporating stories and illustrations into your presentations. It involves two stages. First, have each person in your group tell a story, joke, or other short illustration. Then have everyone brainstorm about different lessons which can be learned from the story. What messages does it have, and what are some examples of topics it could be used to support? After you have tried this, make it harder. Have one person in the group tell a story. Then build on it. Have the next person tell a different type of story which illustrates a similar point. Once a personal anecdote has been used, no one else may use one. Only one nursery rhyme, one story from history, and so on. See how long you can keep going on one topic.

Finding Opportunities: The great thing about impromptu speaking is that you can practice anytime and anywhere. Explain to your parents the meaning of a book you are reading, thinking especially about comparing it to other things. Learn to speak out in group settings such as Sunday School and the classroom. Always be looking for an opportunity to give your opinion and defend it. Seek out chances to practice. Try giving an impromptu speech in the shower (the timing is just about perfect) or in the car. Learn to love reading, and read with an eye for stories and anecdotes which can be incorporated into a speech. Think about the funny stories that have happened in your life. What lessons could be taken from these, and what topics could you plug them into? Becoming an excellent impromptu speaker, as well as an interesting thinker, speaker, and writer in general, will be greatly helped by organizing a mental file from which you can draw.

Impromptu speaking probably sounds like it will be very difficult. You are right about that. However, the skills you gain from this activity can literally change your life. Enjoy.

Part Two: Interpretive Speeches

Introduction to Interpretation

To students just getting started in individual events, the interpretive events can seem like a strange new world that is simultaneously confusing and fascinating. Watching someone practice an interpretation without knowing what they are doing, you may mistake them for being schizophrenic or delusional. The experienced competitor in interpretation becomes amazingly skilled at switching instantaneously from character to character, seamlessly capturing a variety of voices, emotions, and attitudes. If you are a creative person or if you just love to perform, then interpretation will be perfect for you, and will allow you to truly make literature come alive both for yourself and your audience.

"All the world's a stage, and all the men and women merely players."
- Shakespeare

Why Should I Do Interpretation?

Many students gravitate toward interpretation because it is a great outlet for their creativity. Indeed, when you put together an interpretive speech for competition, you get to become the producer, director, and star of your own little show. This will require that you stretch yourself to think about new ways of engaging an audience, as you step into a different world and portray several different characters. Interpretation does not use any props, costumes, setting, or makeup, so it is a special challenge to slip into character. You will discover an artistic side and a

level of creative ingenuity that you never thought you had before.

Interpretation is also great because it helps you to explore your full range as a performer and speaker. As you decide how to represent different characters, you will have to use your voice, your face, and your body to create contrasts and emotions. After doing this, you will find out how much more able you are to bring expression and passion to every other presentation you give. Students who have participated in interpretive speaking events are usually easy to pick out by the enthusiasm and animation they are able to bring to other speeches and projects.

The greatest benefit of doing interpretation, however, is the new depth of appreciation that it gives you for literature. Interpretation makes you a better reader, and helps you to understand how authors and playwrights create story, character, and emotion. When you plan an interpretation, you have to think carefully about what the author was imagining when he or she wrote the piece of literature you are performing. This will help you immeasurably in school, but it will also enrich your life outside of school as you become better at capturing some of the beauty that literature can express.

What is Interpretation?

Perhaps the best and most succinct way to define interpretation is to call it "theatre of the mind." Interpretation is the art of performing a piece of literature so as to capture it in its intellectual, emotional, and aesthetic entirety. If that sounds like a mouthful, then just think of interpretive events as being your chance to step into your favorite play or novel and truly become a part of its world. For the duration of your performance you will become another person, and the success of your presentation depends on how entirely you can step into that person's shoes.

The goal of interpretation is to bring a piece of literature to life for an audience. My father describes this with a simple metaphor. When you do an interpretation, you find a dusty old piece of literature that would be easy to overlook, like a jewel buried in the mud. As you study this literature, it is as if you are polishing the jewel and holding it up in the light so that the audience can see and appreciate every facet of its beauty. By performing the literature in front of an audience, you can help them to appreciate it in a way that they would not have imagined before.

Differences Between Interpretation and Acting:

Many beginning speech competitors have trouble understanding the nature of interpretation, and how it is different from acting. The distinction between these two is subtle but significant, so it is instructive to carefully examine what makes interpretation different from acting in order to gain a clear understanding of the nature of both. First, it is very important to stress that interpretation is absolutely not just "toned-down acting." The interpreter should respond, act, and move almost exactly as the actor does, and trying to distinguish the two by arbitrary limits on motions is oversimplification.

Interpretation differs from acting in its mindset more than anything else. The goal of the actor is to create an accurate representation of a fictional world, complete with sets, props, costumes, makeup, and other actors. For the actor, the audience is simply an invisible spectator, allowed to observe the fictional world as it transpires on stage or screen. Meanwhile, an interpreter has a much less concrete and more evocative task to accomplish. The goal of interpretation is to suggest a fictional world, and actually transport both herself and the audience into the time and place of the story, so much so that the real world is forgotten. While the actor fixes her attention on the real objects being used on stage, the interpreter must focus on mental objects as if they were really there and react accordingly. The interpreter looks into the audience but visualizes the fictional world, allowing the observers to feel as if they too are a part of this world, actually watching events unfold as if they were there.

Different Types of Interpretation:

There are two basic categories of interpretation. The first of these includes the presence of a narrator who actually addresses the audience. This type of interpretation is known as the lyric mode. In the lyric mode, the interpreter may still portray several different characters, and the narrator himself is often a separate character, but most lyric interpretation addresses the audience. In contrast, the dramatic mode of interpretation is where the audience is not addressed and there is not a narrator. In the dramatic mode the competitor may provide some brief narration at the beginning, but most of the speech takes place as if the audience is not really there.

In many leagues, there are specific events for the lyric mode such as prose interpretation and specific events for the dramatic mode such as dramatic interpretation. In other leagues, you may find that all interpretation is lumped together into a few broad categories such as dramatic and humorous interpretation. Make sure you know what is expected of you whenever you enter an event at any speech tournament. In general, the most popular form of interpretation is in the dramatic mode, and the vast majority of interpretive speeches you will see will be without the presence of a narrator.

Preparing an Interpretation

Finding Material: The first thing you will need to do to prepare any interpretive speech is find a good piece of literature to interpret. This is also one of the most difficult and time-consuming tasks of interpretation and it can be frustrating, especially for the beginner. It is definitely worth it to go the extra mile and seek out a piece that you will genuinely enjoy performing. The first place to look for good material is your own memory. Consider any novels or plays or other literature that you have really enjoyed and that have had a significant meaning to you.

Sources: Many interpreters use selections of literature from reading they have done for school, or they take a scene from their favorite book. This is good because you will be able to identify well with the characters and communicate your love for the literature that you are presenting.

As a general rule, the best pieces to interpret are those that are very realistic, that offer believable and compelling characterization and action. You may find some material that has just been written for the purpose of being a short interpretive piece, and does not have fully developed characters. Often, these pieces end up falling flat. They are too syrupy or preachy or shallow and they fail to really draw the audience into the action. Consistently the most successful interpretations are those of the highest literary quality, because they have more substance for the interpreter to work with.

You are required to use literature from a published source, which rules out short skits and stories that might be found on a web site or a cassette tape. You are not allowed to use scripts that you have taken from media, such as movies or television and radio shows. This is because interpretation of media captured scripts is usually nothing more than mimicking what the actors did in the original performance. In interpretation, the emphasis is on using your own creativity to plan a performance, not copying something that has already been done.

High quality plays are a great place to find material. Classic writers such as Moliére, Marlowe, and even Sophocles can be used with great success, and *Cyrano de Bergerac* is one of many fertile sources for humorous interpreters. The plays of Shakespeare are probably used more than any other single author, because they are filled with wonderful characters and excellent dramatic and humorous scenes. For many students, however, modern material is generally more effective than pieces from older literature. This is true for a number of reasons, but the central point

"To read means to borrow; to create out of one's readings is paying off one's debts."
- Christoph Lichtenberg

95

is that we moderns tend to be separated from the classics by a number of barriers, such as language, culture, and life situation. It might be easier for you to understand and interpret a piece of literature that is set in a more recent and familiar time and place.

Look to such great modern playwrights as Eugene O'Neill, Arthur Miller, or Neil Simon, among many others. The most important question to ask yourself when analyzing a potential piece is whether or not you can truly identify with it and visualize it in your mind. The success of your speech will depend on your ability to step into another world, and that is most possible when the literary world has been constructed by a true master. You might want to check out some live performances or filmed versions of famous plays to stoke your imagination about what you can do with the literature.

In addition to plays, novels and stories can provide good scenes for you to interpret. Many authors have a wonderful sense of character and dialogue, which you can craft into a winning performance. Some of my favorites for this include Mark Twain, Oscar Wilde, and Jane Austen. I have seen students interpret powerful scenes from modern classics such as *To Kill a Mockingbird*, *All Quiet on the Western Front*, and *Awakenings*. You probably have favorites of your own that would work just as well.

For younger interpreters and beginning students, children's literature can be wonderful to interpret. The books of Dr. Seuss and the stories of A.A. Milne have some great scenes and characters that can be very fun to interpret. Also, because new students often have a difficult time choosing a short scene from a long novel or play, you might want to start with a short story that is easier to get a handle on. You can find lots of great literature online - one of my favorite sites for this is called Bibliomania (www.bibliomania.com).

Characteristics of a Good Selection: The main character in most winning interpretive speeches is sympathetic, and undergoes some moral victory or growth over the course of the piece. Most audiences simply will not respond well to speeches in which the main character is some sort of sinister villain engaged in evil or immoral acts. People also tend not to appreciate drama that results in the good guy losing somehow, or being overcome by temptation or outside forces. Try to stay with pieces that have a theme that is uplifting, and a clear message about life and the human condition. This does not mean that you should shy away from tackling difficult issues, or even from having your main character die at the end. There should just be a feeling of accomplishment at the end.

For example, the end of *A Tale of Two Cities* definitely tackles some tough issues, such as sacrifice and tragedy, and the hero does die. This book still has an uplifting end, however, because something bigger is accomplished through what happens to the hero, so this might be a great scene to perform as an interpretation. At the end of your speech, the audience should feel as if they have seen a good character accomplish something, and win a victory even if it is only a moral one. This can also be accomplished through having the main character learn an important lesson. Some literature shows a character learning something by experiencing a tragic or difficult chain of events. You can use this sort of literature as well, as long as the audience gets the message.

As you evaluate material, you should always consider how well you will be able to do the characters. While there may be some three hundred pound guys that can play Tinkerbell, I still have not seen one. I have seen a number of interpretations in which the interpreter was not at all appropriate for the characters, and the result is almost always unintentional laughter. No matter how talented you are, it does not make any sense to try to portray someone who is completely out of your character. Determine what your strengths are. You may have a special knack for playing senior citizens, or, as is the

"Literature adds to reality, it does not simply describe it... It irrigates the deserts that our lives have already become."
- C.S. Lewis

case with one friend of mine, mentally disabled people. Seek out plays that feature the kind of characters you know you can perform.

Also consider how many characters the piece requires you to take on. While a well-developed monologue can be incredibly difficult to do, the fact is that it will not be as impressive to the judges as the interpretation that incorporates several fully realized characters. On the other hand, very few students can find it within themselves to distinguish between ten or twelve different characters. You will be best served by finding a piece that has two to five characters, all of which you feel comfortable with portraying. This does not mean that monologues can not win tournaments, and many have, just as many students have done very well with many, many characters. However, as a general rule, two to five characters are ideal.

Take an active role in selecting interpretive material by seeking out and reading plays, soliciting recommendations, and keeping your eyes and ears open. Approach people you know who are familiar with drama, and see if they have any advice. Examine anthologies of plays until you find something that catches your eye. Think through books you have read that were especially meaningful to you. Eventually, you will read or see a piece that you will just know is perfect for you. Do not settle for anything that does not capture you. Remember that you will be working with this piece for a long time, and you need to enjoy it. You will only be able to effectively interpret scenes and characters that you can relate to, so make a special effort to find material of sufficient literary merit that works for you.

A final thing to account for as you look for the perfect piece is the acceptability of content and language. You never want to perform material that will offend or embarrass the listeners, or that is uncomfortable or graphic in content. This certainly is not a model of Christlike communication, and should be absolutely avoided. On the other hand, the very nature of drama is to tackle difficult subject matter, and it seems like almost every great play ends in murder or suicide. Sometimes, a certain line may be absolutely necessary to the dramatic impact of a piece. Imagine Lady Macbeth saying "Out, silly spot." It does not quite work.

While I would encourage you to never ever use one of the seven words you can never say on television, there are very few absolute rules outside of that. You must judge each script on a case by case basis, deciding if its literary merit and moral message outweighs any possibly objectionable content. A simple litmus test is to imagine yourself performing the piece in front of your grandmother. If you could not do that, it may not be the best selection, because you never know just who your judge will be.

Cutting a Script for Interpretation: Once you have found a play that you absolutely love, you may have difficulty actually choosing a ten minute portion of it for your script. The process of creating a ten minute selection is known as cutting, and should be done with great care. Your final cutting should have a clear beginning, middle, and end, and anyone who has never seen or read the play should still be able to follow and understand it without difficulty. You can accomplish this either by picking out and interpreting the climactic scene of the play, or by picking out a subplot that runs throughout the play, and turning it into the focus of your performance.

It is a good idea to cut down to a scene that runs to about nine minutes in length. You want to allow enough extra time for adding movement and pauses, as well as audience reaction and anything unexpected that might happen during your speech. The cutting process can be difficult, and you may be required to make some difficult decisions about what to get rid of and what to keep, but it is imperative that you have a script that is well within the time limits. The last thing you want is a performance that feels overly rushed.

The chief quality shared by all good cuttings is seamlessness. You want the audience to feel as if your performance fits together smoothly, and not to get the impression that it is a disconnected collection of different scenes that you have thrown together. Eliminate anything that is extraneous or unnecessary to your focus, such as minor characters and subplots. Avoid having a cutting that is too messy, with a complex array of different developments and characters, or several scene changes. If you must use material from more than one scene in the play, consider adding some bridge material so that the transition is smooth. Cut your piece down to only what is essential to the development of the scene you are focusing on, and eliminate anything else that distracts from that end.

The general rule for cutting interpretations is that you are allowed to add at least 150 of your own words. Most speech leagues allow for this. The first thing that most interpreters add is a brief introduction that introduces the author and piece of literature that is being performed, along with any background information that might be helpful to the audience. You should make sure you do this near the beginning of your speech.

In addition to an introduction, you might want to add a few lines to assist with clarity. If you have put together several scenes, you can insert some lines into one of the characters' mouths to help smooth over the transition. If you are performing from a novel and you would like to eliminate the narrator, you can change the third person to first person. "He stared longingly at the doughnut in his hand" can be changed to "I stared longingly at the doughnut in my hand." You can also eliminate minor characters by giving their lines to one of the major characters. The only limitation on what you can do is the 150 word rule.

Script Analysis: Upon cutting your script, the next step toward creating an effective interpretation is to explore and examine the selection until you have a

Bad Advice:
"If the audience never understands the plot, it can be counted on to be attentive to the very end."
- Benedetto Marcello

100

complete understanding of every nuance and detail. This is probably the most time-consuming part of preparing an interpretation, and yet the process of script analysis will enrich your presentation immeasurably. Only by conducting a detailed examination of the selection can you equip yourself to bring its story and characters alive.

Good script analysis must by necessity begin with a good script. For the purposes of this discussion, we will assume that you have been able to locate a script that you enjoy, that is of sufficient depth and literary quality, and that you have also taken the time to read the entire play from which the cutting is made. This last step is very important, and should always be done to gain a better appreciation of the setting of your interpretation. Good literature requires a certain level of commitment and careful reading and re-reading. As you do this, there are five steps you should take towards understanding your script.

Step 1: Read and Reread the Script Aloud

First, you should spend some time reading your speech out loud. Before doing anything else, simply go into a room by yourself and read your script out loud several times. Do not necessarily try to do voices, or anything too special, just listen for the rhythm of the words and the development of the plot. You will be surprised at how much this helps you grasp the piece. You will find yourself slipping into the characters despite yourself, and quickly memorizing the script by the time you have read it aloud only four or five times.

This is also the chance for easy troubleshooting. If there are any words that you have difficulty pronouncing, or that you have any doubt whatsoever as to the meaning of, look them up. Leave nothing to chance, but make sure that you have a complete understanding of what is happening in the script. Shakespeare can be notorious for throwing off interpreters, because many of the words he uses have changed in meaning over the years. Be careful at this stage of analysis, because nothing will be more embarrassing than putting in hours of work on your speech and then discovering that you have completely misunderstood the topic.

You also want to begin to think through double meanings or unspoken ideas that are present in the script. Remember that the lines the characters say are only half of the story. You want to examine what they are really thinking and feeling and what they mean when they deliver these lines. You should begin to get a sense for the interaction of the characters as you read the script aloud.

Step 2: Create Character Profiles

The next stop on the road to interpretive success is to go through the entire piece of literature from which your selection is taken and look for background information on the characters you are playing. Find every single fact that you can about each character that you are portraying and write it down. Prepare a set of character profiles, each of which should be quite long for a well-written work of literature. Start by looking for what the author or playwright tells you about the character, in both the introduction to the play and the stage notes. Look for physical descriptions, character traits, life history, and motivations. Look at anything which the character says about himself, and how other characters describe him as well. Write out a complete description of every last thing you know about the character, until you feel as if you know him personally. Having this knowledge will make you much more able to truly evoke that character in the minds of your audience.

In addition to creating a detailed profile of your characters, you should spend some time mapping out the relationships between characters. As I am sure you are well aware, real life relationships are complex, and so are relationships in well-written literature. Spend some time carefully reading the play to uncover the exact way in which the different characters interrelate. Once again, be very specific and make a special effort to capture all the nuances. For example, it is not enough to say that Jocasta is the mother of Oedipus. This obviously does not even begin to describe their relationship, and gives you no idea of how to portray either character. Figure out what each character thinks about the other, and how those thoughts affect the way they act toward each other. Look for specifics such as mixtures of love and hate, the way attitudes change over the course of your selection, and the history of the various relationships. Write all of this down, and use it as you interpret the material.

Step 3: Translate the Character Profiles into Physical Characteristics

After preparing these character profiles, you should begin considering how to communicate the reality of these characters physically. You must translate the verbal descriptions of the characters into your own three-dimensional behavior in your interpretation. The secret to creating great characters is in the details. How would this person stand, or talk, or move? Take into consideration the person's age, gender, personality, and habits. For an older character, you might stoop over, move slowly and carefully, and talk in a thin, weary voice.

The best way to develop characters is to simply observe how real people behave. Concentrate on every little thing you can to give flesh and blood to you characters. Ask yourself what is different between the way aggressive and passive people respond to adversity, how often people blink when they are nervous, and how you hold your hands and change your posture when embarrassed. The more real life you can put into your performance, the better communication you will offer, and the more rich and engaging your interpretation will be.

Spend plenty of time creating your characters. Each person should have his own voice, posture, and attitudes. It might be helpful to take each character in your script and ask yourself what real people he reminds you of. Use the characteristics of that per-

"The art of acting presupposes three phases: understanding a part, intuiting a part, and contemplating the essence of a part."
- Franz Grillparzer

son to help yourself imagine and get into your character fully.

Step 4: Plot Out the Narrative Flow

While the previous two activities concentrate on the characters in your speech, the fourth step is more about the overall flow of the script. Examine your selection and the overall play from which it is taken for background, conflict, climax, resolution, humor, message, and feeling. Every selection should contain every one of these, and it is up to you to find it and figure out how to capture it for the audience. Initially, figure out the background and setting of the selection, and what has been happening to lead up to the moment of drama. Identify and describe in your own words what the central conflict in the episode is. This could be a conflict between two or more characters, or an internal conflict in the life of one character.

All good drama should carry its conflict toward a definite climax near the end, after which the tension is resolved in the lives of the characters and in the mind of the audience. You should know the exact moment when the climax occurs, and how this changes every character in your performance. Plot out and write down exactly what happens during the piece, with an eye toward making your speech crackle with anticipation, suspense, and a crisp, clear payoff at the end.

Several other factors are crucial to successful drama, and these may require some deeper digging. One essential point is that every single scene, no matter how serious or tragic, contains some humor, and this is a definite reflection of real life. Closely examine your script for the lines that will bring a smile to the face of your audience, and make sure you do not let them get lost in an attempt to be overly tragic or dramatic. A second component of good drama is the message which it conveys. Dorothy Sayers, the British author, once made the profound observation that "The dogma is the drama." This means that it is the conflict between right and wrong which captures the audience, and all good drama should contain a message. The final and most important factor in meaningful drama is the recreation of true human feeling through the characters. This is the bottom line, and you absolutely must feel the emotions of the conflict along with your characters, in order to make these feelings genuine to the audience. Every single good selection will be faithful to the way human beings feel, react, and behave, and the only successful interpretation is the one in which this feeling truly comes alive.

Step 5: Build the Subtext

This final method of analyzing your script is one of the most important tools employed by every great actor; building the subtext. However, it is time-consuming and many students do not want to put out the amount of effort which it takes. I can only encourage you that doing the work of creating a subtext will add immeasurably to your performance. The difference between the emotional impact of a piece with or without a subtext is like the difference between a cap gun and a stick of dynamite.

A subtext is a written representation of what is happening in the minds of your characters during the course of the script. Different interpreters have different styles of creating a subtext, but the most common format is to make a large piece of paper with five columns. The actual spoken text of the script goes into the first column, word for word exactly as it will be presented in the speech. The other four columns will contain the thoughts, memories, senses, and intentions of the characters who are speaking the text. Thus, for each spoken line of dialogue, you will be able to scan across all five columns for in depth information about what that line really means. Utilize all the other script analysis you have done as you make your subtext.

In the column immediately next to the actual text, you should write down what the character who is speaking each line is thinking. Across from the line of dialogue, note the mental state of the character.

When you do this carefully, you will quickly discover how often the character is thinking something completely different from what she is saying, and in fact many times the two are complete opposites. When asked how they are doing, people will usually say they are fine, even when they have never felt worse in their life. You need to train yourself to recognize this in your subtext, and represent it so that the audience will recognize what each character is thinking.

The third column should be used for the memories of the character delivering the line. Some interpreters choose to group this with the first column, but there are some differences between the two. Basically, memories encompass all the life history that has gone into the character leading up to this moment. You should consider what the character has experienced in the specific relationship that is being discussed, what important events have recently happened in the character's life, and any other memories that could be impacting the character's behavior. This will provide enhanced depth to both your and your audience's understanding of what is really happening in the drama.

In the fourth column, you should write down what things the character is sensing as she speaks. This is one of the easier ones, simply requiring you to look at the text and determine the things that the character sees, feels, hears, smells, or tastes. Whatever it is that this character is aware of, you will need to be mentally aware of in your performance as well, so make a note of it.

This includes any "stage business," which just means the activities the character might be involved in. Activities can include ironing clothes, pouring a drink, plumping the pillows of a hospital patient, and so on. Do not make these activities too elaborate, but do include them because they contribute to making your performance realistic. Sometimes the activities of the character will be mentioned in the literature, but many times you will have to imagine what he or she might be doing.

The final column of your subtext sums up the other four, as it should include the intentions and actions of the characters involved. This is where you analyze what the character actually wants from who she is talking to, or what she is trying to accomplish by her action. Everything that is said in your script springs from some motivation or desire, and you need to figure out what the motivation is and how to depict it.

The process of creating a subtext is the key to gaining a complete understanding of precisely what your script is really all about. It is a long process, but it will enrich your characterization immeasurably. This step is the culmination of all your script analysis, and it is a method that has been used by the very best actors for generations. By the time you have completed the five steps of successful script analysis, you will have pages of detailed notes and be prepared to recreate a scene of such feeling, vitality, and meaning that your audience truly will be swept away by the theatre of the mind.

Preparing to Perform:

When the selection and cutting are completed, and the process of script analysis has been done, you are ready to begin practicing your speech. As you begin to actually develop the performance, make good use of all the notes and preparation you have made, and use your subtext and character profiles extensively. You should have a very clear picture of what each character looks and acts like in your mind, and the goal is to represent that with your body.

Obviously, no amount of character work will do any good if the audience cannot tell the characters apart, so your biggest job will be to make clear distinctions between characters. One common technique is to assign a different vocal register to each character. A little girl would be a soprano, an older woman could be an alto, young men would be tenors, and so forth. This doesn't mean that you should sing the lines, but that you should alter the pitch of your

Sidebar: Learning From The Best

In order to deliver a good interpretation, you will need to switch between several different characters. This means developing a set of unique qualities for each character.

A few Hollywood actors are especially good at portraying a wide range of characters. It can be helpful to watch several movies with the same actor to see how one person can play several different roles convincingly.

One great example of this is Humphrey Bogart, who plays three very different characters in the movies *Casablanca*, *The Treasure of the Sierra Madre*, and *The Caine Mutiny*.

If you watch these three films, you can see how Bogart adjusted his voice, posture, facial expressions, and use of hands to become convincing in each role.

Other actors who have played a wide range of roles include Marlon Brando, Tom Hanks, and Robin Williams. Each of these actors commits his entire body to every role that he plays.

By studying the professionals, you can learn how to create captivating characters.

voice for each character. Also, each character should have a distinct posture, set of mannerisms, and possibly a unique accent as well. Be very careful, however, about turning characters into caricatures. If your interpretation descends into superficiality or stereotypes, it will not be appreciated by the audience. This is true even of humorous interpretation, where the funniest characters are the ones that are realistic and that actually remind the audience of people they know.

A second way to create distinctions between characters is to give each one a different focal point. The focal point is where you are looking in the room when the character is speaking. You need to actually pick a spot in the room, and mentally place whatever the character is looking at on that spot. If you do not have a specific focal point, your character's focus will be inconsistent, and the audience will think she is watching a fly dart around. When recreating a dialogue, have one character facing slightly to your left, and another facing slightly to your right. Visualize the characters standing facing each other, but only make a slight turn each way, projecting along two different lines in a V shape. For more characters, simply add different focal points. The key is to keep the focal points consistent, and always have one character facing in the same direction.

Do not deliver a line of dialogue facing sideways, and then step across into the opposite position and deliver the other character's line facing sideways the other way. This looks ridiculous, and only serves to make the audience angry at you. In fact, the shifting between characters should be done without any steps whatsoever. Stay in the same place and change your posture and focal point to change character. The only time you should actually take a step is when one of the characters takes a step, or to signify a change in scene. Stepping from character to character looks bad - the switch should be instant and complete.

You will need to practice, practice, practice in order to refine your presentation. The audience must be able to distinguish between characters based on voice alone, on stance alone, and on focal points alone. When these three are combined, there should be no doubt as to which character is which. Therefore, the worst thing you can do is a slow or incomplete character transition. When you have the voice of one character but the stance and focal points of another, the audience will be confused. A shift in character needs to be absolute and instant, with no blending or mixing.

It is difficult to put a whole lot of interaction between characters into a single interpretation, unless you are extremely talented at shaking your own hand or kissing yourself. This means that you will have to emphasize the relationships between characters through your posture and voice. Have a dominant character tower and shout, while a timid one cowers and pouts. The best interpreters use their focal points and expressions so perfectly that you can almost see them shrinking and growing physically as they switch characters, and every single aspect of their body and the way they move is different. You can accomplish this level of realism by carefully observing people, especially people who are similar to the way you imagine your characters. Try to capture all the little details, such as trademark gestures, facial expressions, and reactions, and incorporate them into your interpretation of the character.

An interpreter must strive to become transparent to the audience. When we see a great performance of drama, the performer quite literally disappears, and we see not an actor playing a character, but the actual character. The more completely the interpreter is transformed into the role, the better. Great interpretation occurs when the audience no longer sees or hears the interpreter but sees and hears the scene itself.

Introducing Yourself:
In competition, you will not want to go up to the front of the room and just dive right into your

piece without any explanation or setup. You need to devise a short but attention-grabbing introduction that lays all the necessary groundwork for your speech. The introduction will be the very first thing which your audience sees, so you must make it vivid and interesting. During an interpretation round, you will usually be speaking right after someone who has made a powerful impression on the audience, and you need to draw the attention back to yourself rather quickly.

One of the most popular ways to do this is to begin with a short teaser from the play itself. This is just a few highly dramatic lines from the play, usually delivered by the main character. Other interpreters choose to open with some shocking or subversive statement or question that catches the audience off guard, a tactic that can be very effective if your script is about some tragic or gruesome event such as a murder. You could also begin by singing some lines from a familiar song, such as an old spiritual to introduce a piece about slavery, or by describing in your own words the setting of your scene.

After catching the attention of the audience with one of these methods, make sure you give the essentials, the title and the author of your selection. Every league requires that you introduce these things, but never simply announce them in a monotone at the beginning. Without some teaser or attention-getter at the very beginning, your introduction will put the audience right to sleep. Also, the introduction should never last more than about thirty seconds before you get into the meat of your scene. Simply get the audience interested, tell them the essentials, and get started. Nothing will kill interest faster than a long, detailed introduction. If your piece requires too much background information, then consider editing or changing the selection.

Practicing:
In order to improve your interpretation, you will need plenty of feedback from other people. You should perform it many times in front of different

people. Your parents, your speech coach or teacher, other members of your club or class, and especially judges at tournaments can give you valuable comments to help you to improve. Never ignore or be hurt by criticism, but use it as an opportunity to improve. Think about what you could change to help the audience to appreciate your speech even more.

This goes especially for any comments or suggestions that you receive from several different people. This usually means there is a real weakness that you should work on. In order to achieve your highest potential, you should always be willing to tinker with your performance, constantly fine-tuning it with each new time you practice.

Ideas for Improving

There are several great ways to practice your interpretive skills, and they can be a lot of fun both to participate in and to watch. Get together with some other interpreters in your school or club, or simply practice with your family. Enjoy yourself doing these activities, and remember that one of their chief benefits is getting you to overcome any inhibitions about performing in front of people. Do not allow yourself to be crippled by embarrassment, but learn to be comfortable playing a number of different characters.

Perhaps the best activity is to simply experiment with the stance and voice of a wide variety of different characters. Try to create a cynical college student, a military general, a football player, a beauty contestant, and any other character you can think of simply by the way you stand. Add in the voice and facial expressions, and see if you can get your audience to guess what you are trying to be. Try characters that are similar to you, and those that are your complete opposites. Imitate celebrities or politicians, and figure out exactly what aspects of the way they behave make them recognizable. Act out the same activity, such as coughing, answering the phone, or meeting some one new, with several characters, and experiment with how they would do these things differently.

After experimenting with different characters, begin to explore different emotions and attitudes. Take a rather innocuous line, such as "We have had some interesting weather lately," or "I think he is in the garage," and deliver it in several ways, each for a different emotion. Deliver the line as if you are annoyed, heartbroken, happy, bored, confused, terrified, and so forth. Vary the speed at which you speak, your tone of voice, your pitch, and all other vocal characteristics to evoke different moods. After doing this, try to create the same emotions with your facial expressions alone, without saying anything at all. Have your friends, coach, or family try to guess what emotion you are conveying just by looking at your face.

One of the best ways to improve your interpretation is to videotape yourself and watch yourself perform. This way, you can actually see whether or not your characters are coming across the way that you intend them to. Videotape is an excellent way to expose little problems of which you may be entirely unaware until you see them.

Finally, put all of these things together. Take a single line that is not very meaningful in and of itself, and deliver it as a number of characters, each character saying it from several different emotions. You will amaze yourself at how much variety you can squeeze out of a single spoken line. Continue to stretch yourself, explore your strengths and weaknesses, and figure out what characters you are good at, and which ones you need to work on. One idea is to fill a jar with character types, another with actions, and a third with different emotions. Pull a slip of paper from each jar, and act out that character doing that activity with that emotion.

Have fun transforming yourself into different people, and performing in front of an audience. As you practice more and more, you will continue discovering little ways to alter your body and voice to create a larger variety of characters. You will learn how posture and facial expressions can communicate volumes about an individual's personality, and how to capture these in their entirety. In the end, you will experience the satisfaction that comes from making art come alive.

Dramatic Interpretation

Dramatic interpretation is "theater of the mind." This event is a true channel for your creative energies. It provides a beautiful outlet to understand and convey the wide range of human emotion and experience. There is great truth in the idea that the philosopher and the thinker can only deal with a part of life, while the poet, the actor, and the artist can create a much deeper, true, and vibrant picture of humanity. Humans will never be impacted by simple rhetoric nearly as much as they will be by drama, which makes dramatic interpretation one of the most powerful of all the individual speaking events.

It can be quite an exciting experience to participate in dramatic interpretation. If you are the creative type, you will love the opportunity to literally become a character or group of characters, to wholeheartedly jump into their world and become a part of it. Interpreting a piece is an interesting challenge usually requiring you to portray several different characters without the aid of props, costumes, or anything but your own body. This feat takes no small amount of creativity and ingenuity. However, you don't have to be overwhelmingly artistic or imbued with superb dramatic talent to be good at this event. The best interpretations simply offer a piece of the human condition, and the most effective way to do this is by genuinely identifying with your characters.

"The play's the thing wherein I'll catch the conscience of the king."
- Shakespeare

Learning to relate to and understand the motivations, emotions, and personalities of other people is an immensely valuable personal quality. Dramatic interpretation gives you a vehicle to do this. It also allows you to participate in the arts and to develop your own creativity. From choosing a piece of literature, to cutting that piece to fit your time limits, to acting out and delivering the interpretation, this event makes you the producer, director, and star of your own performance. The only limitation is a lack of creativity.

How it Works in Competition

In a nutshell, a dramatic interpretation is an attempt to portray the thoughts, emotions, ideas, and purposes of the author of a work of literature by acting out a piece from that work. The speaker has ten minutes to convey this message, including whatever introductory or transitional materials are included. Interpretation is best described as "theatre of the mind," which means no costumes or props or anything extraneous to the body may be used. Using voice, gesture, and facial expression alone, the speaker should strive to carry the listener away mentally to the time and place of the story.

The criteria for judging dramatic interpretation take the entire presentation into account. Speakers are judged on their selection of material, their ability to depict mood, character, and emotion, and the dramatic interest and cohesiveness of the overall creation. An excellent interpretation should hold the attention of the audience, faithfully recreate the author's intent, and accurately portray some real and meaningful human emotion.

Preparing a Dramatic Interpretation

Putting together a dramatic interpretation is a long process that involves a wide variety of jobs. You will need to decide what piece you would like to interpret and cut the piece for dramatic effect and to fit the time limit. Then you will have to memorize the entire speech and plan out the blocking and staging for it. You must quite literally become your character or characters and learn to step into their personalities, voices, and mannerisms instantly. Finally, the entire piece is put together, taking into consideration character interaction, dramatic high points and flow, and appropriate use of your body.

Finding Material:

This can be the most difficult part of an interpretation, and there are many things you should consider.

Content: There are no absolute or specific rules governing content, but you want to be very careful about having acceptable material. You should never use a script containing any of the seven words you can never say on television or use any particularly gratuitous descriptions. However, there is no litmus test as to whether a piece can be performed or not, and a student's ideas about what is acceptable could be very different from what an adult thinks. The solution is simple. Before deciding for sure on a piece, run it by as many responsible adults as you can: your parents, your coach, and anyone else who is willing. Remember you will be performing this in front of a wide variety of people whom you do not know, so make sure you are very comfortable with it. It's probably a good idea not to push the envelope too much. You want your material to be well received, not protested.

Timing: Another thing to keep in mind as you look for material is the ten minute time limit. No matter how hard you try, or how fast you talk, you won't be able to squeeze the entire length of Hamlet into an interp. When deciding what passages to keep and what to cut for your piece, keep it simple. Too much complexity or too many subplots can kill your performance. At the other extreme, make sure that the action is self-explanatory, and don't cut so much that your piece lacks any sense of dramatic completeness. Absolutely nothing ruins a good interpretation quite so quickly as a long boring introduction.

Characters: There are several issues here. It is of utmost importance that you can become the characters in the piece. While the talent of each student will vary, a petite, soft-voiced girl will probably have trouble with playing General Patton, and a bulky, throaty guy should stay as far away as possible from the Fairy Queen. Also, you are just one person, and maintaining a distinction between characters is imperative. This means that having twenty different characters is probably a bad idea, as there are only so many different ways to alter your voice and contort your body. Think carefully before choosing a monologue, however. Judges are impressed by students who can create several distinct characters and the interaction between them. This doesn't mean that monologues are always a bad idea, but be sure you have one which allows you to showcase the whole depth and emotional range of your ability.

"A talent for drama is not a talent for writing, but is an ability to articulate human relationships."
- Gore Vidal

Dramatic Impact: This is the single most important criteria for your selection. You want something that is self-contained with a beginning, middle, and end, or, more accurately, a set-up, a climax, and a conclusion. The piece should present a conflict and resolve it while communicating some truth or value. Additionally, you should never choose a piece that does not interest you but stick to material that captures your imagination. Are you excited about performing this? You want something that will grab an audience and provide a memorable and moving experience for the observer.

The key to doing this is to find literature that is compelling. Ideally, there is a moral or actual victory that is accomplished or at least a point to the piece. If the characters feel pain, it must be believable and felt by the audience. Sometimes a touch of humor is helpful as a tool for accomplishing this, because there is humor in even the most serious of themes. In order for your speech to have any real impact, the audience needs to care and be able to find some value in watching the suffering the characters are undergoing.

Compelling literature revolves around three elements; story, character, and emotion. The basic story line should have a beginning, in which the characters are introduced and the audience is shown how they relate to each other and what their situation is. This is followed by a middle, in which the primary conflict of the scene is established and allowed to build to a climax. After this, the end of the story should resolve the conflict and give a picture of how the characters have learned or grown. Running through the beginning, middle, and end should be genuine emotions and a clear moral context for the audience to identify with.

Becoming a Character: To have a truly effective interpretation, you must be able to enter an entirely different time, place, and personality. There are a number of ways to develop a character. First, for each character in your selection, you need to have a different voice, posture, mood, and other distinguishing characteristics. Distinction between characters is crucial, so make sure the audience will have no trouble following you as you switch from person to person. When interpreting several different characters, make each character look toward a different spot in the room. These spots are called points of reference or focal points. For example, during a dialogue angle your body and look thirty to forty-five degrees one way for the first character and the same angle in the other direction for the second, forming a "V" shape facing the audience.

As you decide what each character should look and sound like, carefully study the piece of literature you are interpreting. Analyze what motivates each character and figure out his or her general attitude toward life, the other characters, and the events in your scene. Think about ages, occupations, and places of origin. An elderly character might have a stooped posture, a Texan could talk with a Southern drawl. A helpful tool can be to imagine you are being asked to cast a movie of your passage. Decide which actors you would put in each role, and what it is about them that reminds you of the character.

If a movie of the script has been made, watch it and consider what you like or don't like about the portrayals. Be cautious of this, however, because you do not want to just imitate the actors in the movie. Always make sure that your own creativity is on display when you are doing an interpretation. Maybe one character's personality reminds you of someone you know, and you could use some of that person's characteristics. It is important to think about what personalities the people in your piece would have if you met them. Practice personifying them.

The final step in becoming a character is to capture emotions. Think in depth about what this person is experiencing. If you have ever faced a situation like this, how did you feel, and how did you respond? Mentally place yourself in the situation and project the events of the drama into your real-life surroundings. If the character's mother is dying, picture your own mother dying. If the character is being betrayed by a close friend, picture yourself in that situation or remember when something like that has happened to you.

The impact your presentation will have is directly proportional to the amount of feeling you can invest in it. When performing, don't try to act like a character but actually become that character so his or her reactions are at one with your own. Your ultimate goal is to disappear into another person's personality, emotions, and actions so completely that both you and the audience are transported into that person's world.

Staging and Preparation: Your interpretation needs to be perfectly prepared and choreographed down to the smallest detail. At a competition, it is easy to tell which speakers are just winging their staging and who has carefully considered each move and gesture. Plotting out the staging is much easier once you have developed your characters. Go through the piece line by line, considering how each person would deliver the line. Take a pen and mark up your script, writing in pauses, places where you will walk, and other stage instructions. If you chose a passage from a play, there are probably some staging directions written in, so take these into account.

Pay special attention to the dramatic high points. Every good dramatic interpretation has a "moment of truth" when everything hangs in the balance. You should plan accordingly and figure out how to make this climax capture the minds of the audience. Have your coach watch you, paying attention to every detail. The final result should be a performance that is precisely timed and choreographed.

Humorous Interpretation

The chief goal of a humorous interpretation is to get the audience to laugh. Most people, or at least most of the ones whom I have met, enjoy laughing, so this is consistently one of the most popular events to watch and to participate in. However, it is also one of the most difficult to do well. Finding truly funny material to interpret can be quite a task, and the only thing more difficult than finding the material is delivering it in a funny way. One of the toughest speaking situations imaginable is when you try to elicit laughter and no one even smiles. You need to pour all of your energy into a humorous interpretation to separate the listeners from their inhibition and draw out the laughter. When this happens, no other speaking experience is more thrilling.

Preparing a Humorous Interpretation

A humorous interpretation requires the same amount of preparation as a dramatic interpretation and most of the same advice applies. Nevertheless, several differences should be considered.

Perhaps the toughest part of a humorous interpretation is locating good, solid material. The chief criteria for choosing what to perform should be how funny it is. The perfect piece should make you laugh out loud as you read it, and should continue to amuse you even when you read it the second, third,

"Everything is funny so long as it is happening to somebody else."
- Will Rogers

and fifteenth times. In addition to this, an interpretation must actually be an interpretation and not just a stand-up comedy routine. You are interpreting humorous characters and events, not just telling jokes. This means that, as funny as they may be, David Letterman's monologues and Dave Barry's columns are usually not good material for a humorous interpretation.

In the area of content, there is a very fine line you must tread. In humorous interpretation, even more than in dramatic interpretation, you should aim at being as clean as possible. Certain issues and references can and should be brought up in a fictional context for the purpose of creating meaningful drama that speaks about the state of humanity, but the same sort of material is not appropriate just to get a laugh. Actually, this does not create too much of a problem. Believe it or not, the funniest stuff is also the cleanest, and material that relies on bawdy shock value for laughter is usually not truly funny at all.

Before finally deciding on a piece, you should also weigh how much of an opportunity it gives you to showcase your abilities. Although it is of great importance that you choose something funny, judges are specifically to judge the quality of the interpretation, not how funny the student's selection is. A piece may be hilarious, but severely limited in its range. Pick something you can have fun portraying and that allows you to create interesting characters and a complete performance at the same time.

The key to a good humorous interpretation is to put in plenty of your own ideas. Very few scripts are funny simply based on what they say, so it is up to you to draw out the potential for humor that every script has. Good comedy comes not so much from the action of the characters as from way that they react to each other. You will get just as many laughs from a good facial expression in response to something as you will from lots of over the top choreography.

124

Think about how you can make your speech funnier. Every humorous interpretation should be steadily improved over the course of an entire season. You should be constantly thinking about how to add physical moments or facial expressions that add to the power of your interpretation.

After you have chosen what to interpret, the same general guidelines apply as in dramatic interp. The only difference is you should plan the staging and characters of your speech with an eye towards laughter as opposed to drama. There is more room for broad characterizations and over-the-top staging. Practice extensively in front of an audience until you are comfortable with everything, and practice which kinds of delivery will get the biggest laughs. Pay special attention to comedic timing and facial expression. These will make the difference between earning riotous laughter and gaping yawns. Also make sure you can do your piece without laughing or cracking a smile yourself. Composure is of the essence in comedy. Above all, enjoy yourself and your speech. Your enthusiasm will be contagious, making the audience ready to laugh.

Duo Interpretation

Duo Interpretation is the only individual event that is not, strictly speaking, individual. A duo interpretation is an interpretive speech that is done by two people instead of one. Aside from this, a duo interpretation looks very much like a humorous or a dramatic interpretation. The only wrinkle other than having another person to deal with is that speeches can be either dramatic or humorous. In the same round, one team could be performing *Romeo and Juliet* and the next *The Odd Couple*. This makes for an interesting event which best rewards the pair that works successfully together to portray a variety of emotions.

It can be more fun to work with a partner than to work alone, which means that you can really enjoy preparing a duo interpretation. This also means that you will have to learn about teamwork and you will not have complete control over the final decisions about your speech. Duo interpretation requires some unique skills. It provides the opportunity to develop timing and chemistry when performing with two people, providing the ability to capture a broader range of dramatic and comic effects. Because of this, it will challenge you in a different way than the other competitive speech events.

"As iron sharpens iron, so one man sharpens another."
- Proverbs 27:17

How it Works in Competition

Like the other interpretive events, a duo interpretation is a ten minute speech intended to bring literature to life. One of the ways that duo interpretation is separate from acting is that the two performers are not allowed to look at each other or touch each other at any time. This is because you are interpreting and not producing a mini-play. Just as no costumes, props, or other visual aids are allowed, looking at each other is forbidden because it shifts the focus away from the concept of "theatre of the mind." By looking at each other, you would be using the other performer as a visual aid or a prop. The heart of interpretation is the art of capturing a piece of literature without resorting to any artificial aids, including the visual cues of another performer.

Preparing a Duo Interpretation

Script: Just as in the other interpretive events, your first step toward preparing a duo interpretation is to choose a script. The best scripts for duo are dialogues between two characters. Choose a script that gives a good balance between the two main characters, making sure that both performers have a roughly equal role in the presentation. It is possible to achieve this balance even when one speaker has many more lines than the other. In this case, you want to even things out by having the other speaker provide a constant stream of facial expressions, reactions, and physical responses to what the first is saying.

Look for balanced pieces and scripts with a strong dynamic of interaction between the main characters. You also want to use characters that work well for you and your partner. You can use scripts that have more than two characters as well, as long as one or both of you are skilled at convincingly creating good contrasts between characters. The same skills apply to characterization in duo interpretation as in the other interpretive events. Keep your characters clean and well defined.

Blocking: The interaction and movement between characters in duo interpretation is known as blocking. All interpretive speeches require blocking but it is particularly significant in duo, often separating the good speeches from the great. Because you and your partner cannot look at each other, you need to figure out how to relate without that. Certain conventions have been developed by interpreters to assist with the blocking of a duo piece.

For dialogue, the two speakers face straight forward and look directly forward as if the other were standing there facing them. This works only if you exercise complete self-control and absolutely do not allow yourself to so much as glance out of the corner of your eye at where the other person actually is. Try to actually visualize your partner in front of you and talk to that person as if he or she were really facing you.

When the script calls for the two characters to interact physically, timing and self-control become even more critical. For example, if you are supposed to shake hands with each other, each will extend his or her right hand forward into the air, and the hands should move up and down in perfect unison (without looking, remember). If one character is supposed to hand something to the other, that person would hold out his hand as if it contained something, and the other person would reach out and grasp the imaginary object from the air. In order to indicate a change in scene or character, the most common technique is for one person to pass in front of the other with both still facing forward. This does not count as looking at each other.

The best interpretation teams are so synchronized with each other that they can appear to pat each other on the back, kiss, and even stage an elaborate fight scene. No matter how much physical interaction the script calls for, you can create it in a duo interpretation with some creativity. I have seen teams that were so well-practiced that I almost didn't believe my eyes; they genuinely looked like a pair of people normally interacting as they faced each other.

Aside from the special blocking, duo interpretation follows the same pattern as the other interpretive events. The same basic guidelines and rules for improvement apply. The main difference is the increase in the range of scenes you are able to create. With two people, you can bring literature to life in amazing and vibrantly creative new ways. Take advantage of the many different ways you can interact with a partner to create entertaining and dynamic drama.

Prose and Poetry Interpretation

Prose and Poetry Interpretation is the major competitive category that is devoted to interpretation in the lyric mode, which means that the speaker relies on the use of a narrator. In this way, the interpretation of prose and poetry can be thought of as a form of storytelling. The role of the speaker is to bring a piece of literature to life not through dramatically re-enacting it before the audience, but through sharing it interactively with the audience. You may still use characters in an interpretation of prose or poetry, but you focus on telling the story rather than showing it.

How it Works in Competition

In some speech leagues, prose and poetry interpretation does not receive its own category, but is linked with the other forms of interpretation. In some cases, it is referred to as storytelling. Some leagues have a broad general category that puts together prose and poetry interpretation, thematic interpretation, and the interpretation of original work by the speaker. Aside from these variations, the same general rules govern interpretation in the lyric or narrative mode as the rules concerning interpretation in the dramatic mode.

Preparing a Prose or Poetry Interpretation

You should prepare this sort of interpretation in the same way as you would any other interpretation. The same rules of narration, character, and emotion would apply.

Thematic Interpretation

A thematic interpretation is a speech that presents several different works of literature, combining them into a common theme. The literature used should vary and each piece of literature that is introduced should have a new point to add about the theme. A thematic interpretation can be thought of as being like a speech about a subject, with literature being used to illustrate the main points. A competitor can do a thematic interpretation revolving around a theme such as prejudice, love, fire, or war.

How it Works in Competition

Thematic interpretation is usually grouped together with prose and poetry interpretation, even though it can be very different. Competitors are judged not only on the quality of interpretation, but on the originality and thoughtfulness of the overall speech theme. A good thematic interpretation should weave together several different strands of good literature to make one common point. Thus, it is a combination of a platform speech and an interpretive speech.

Preparing a Thematic Interpretation

A thematic interpretation should grow out of your own interests. If you can find several different works of literature that have a common thread binding them together, then you have the working material for a good thematic speech. In thematic interpretation, you write sections that introduce the theme and tie together the different material you are interpreting. The parts that you write are of equal importance to the quality of the literature you interpret

Original Prose and Poetry

Original Prose and Poetry, often referred to as OPP, is interpretation of material that the student has written herself. This may be dramatic or humorous, with or without a narrator. If you are a creative writer and you want to share some of the material that you have written, this is your opportunity to present it. This event can be extremely difficult to judge because it can have so much variety. One speaker may choose to tell a collection of amusing family anecdotes, another may perform a script that he has written, and a third may just want to read some of her poetry. All of these fit into this category.

How it Works in Competition

Very few speech tournaments offer Original Prose and Poetry as a separate event. In most cases, original work by the speaker will placed in the same category as Prose and Poetry Interpretation. Make sure you check the rules of the speech league you are competing in to see whether original work is allowed.

Preparing Original Prose and Poetry

This event has very few guidelines. The only limits are your creativity. This is your chance to explore the challenge of making a presentation out of fictional or dramatic material that you have written for yourself.

Closing Thoughts

This book has discussed many different styles and methods of public speaking, and I hope that at least one or two of them have caught your interest. Even in competition, every public speech is an opportunity to communicate a message, whether you are using the tools of persuasion, the presentation of information, or the interpretation of drama to get your point across. If you use the methods taught in this book, and apply plenty of hard work and practice, you will be amazed by your ability to inspire, motivate, or entertain any audience.

The ultimate purpose of this new ability should always be to bring greater glory to God. It is my hope and prayer that you will realize that competition in individual events is not just another school activity or an opportunity to win trophies. Training in public speaking is training for the real world, and communication with the world is something God calls us to do every single day of our lives.

Your focus in speech should be on being a witness for the truth, and every speech that says something true about the world ultimately reflects the Christian worldview. There are many people in the world who have mastered the art of communication, but are using it to spread lies. Christians should be even more dedicated to pursue excellence in communication, because we have been called to speak the truth.

"Don't let anyone look down on you because you are young, but set an example for the believers in speech, in life, in love, in faith, in purity."
- 1 Timothy 4:12

Part Three: Appendices

Appendix A:
Tournament Time

Your first experience at an individual events tournament will likely seem strange and imposing. There will be many people there who are using new and strange jargon in reference to the numerous different events going on. You may find yourself waiting for a long time before getting a chance to speak, and you will be surrounded by students practicing their speeches by passionately delivering them while facing into the corner of a room or the outside walls. For many people, it is disorienting just to see so many teenagers who are friendly, well dressed, articulate, and serious about achieving excellence. That is not something you see every day. As you gain experience with competitive tournaments, you will grow to love them and the atmosphere of excitement and anticipation that surrounds each one. Before you can do this, however, you need to understand what to expect and how to act in the tournament environment. This chapter will discuss what the average tournament day is like, how the events are judged, and some basic guidelines for dress and etiquette.

A Day in the Life of an Individual Events Tournament

When you first arrive at a tournament in the morning, you will need to register. Depending on the tournament, you will be registering either as an indi-

individual or with your club or school. Usually you will be given a schedule for the tournament and a map of the facility where it is being held, and you should always check these to make sure you will be able to get to the places you need to be at the right time. At most tournaments there will be a short orientation period to cover any unique aspects of that particular tournament and to clarify any questions people may have. After this, you will wait until the first round schedule is posted.

Do not be surprised if you end up waiting quite a while before actually getting a chance to speak. Individual events tournaments are notorious for running behind schedule, due to the complicated scheduling of so many different competitors, judges, and events. Be patient, and use the time to your advantage. The best speakers never miss a final opportunity to practice their presentations, so find an unused stairwell or corner and practice your speech. It may seem odd to stand and deliver a speech to nobody, but it will allow you to concentrate on the little adjustments you need to make in pacing, movement, and gesture to enhance your message. In addition to this, spend some time meeting and talking to new people.

When the round is posted, you need to check for your name or code on the posting sheet, and go to the appropriate room. Postings should clearly indicate the event, the room, and the order of speakers in the round. If you are entered in more than one event, the tournament schedulers should have accounted for this and scheduled you to go early in one event and later in the other. Find the round where you are scheduled to speak the earliest and go there first. After speaking there, make your way to your next event. Judges should be prepared to adjust schedules when necessary to make things run more smoothly.

An individual events round usually consists of six speakers, but can have anywhere from four to eight. Each student will deliver their speech to a

panel of three judges, who will rank the performances from first to last. The judges also provide a
point score to allow for more specific analysis of each
student. The rank determines who performed the
best in the round, and the ranks are added together
over the course of the day. After two or three preliminary rounds, in which every speaker competes,
the top 12 to 16 speakers in each event will progress
to semi-final rounds. Each event will have two rooms
of semi-final rounds.

The top performers in each semi-final round
will progress to a final round, which consists of the
top five to eight speakers in each event. The process
of making it to a semi-final or final round is known
as "breaking," so every competitor wants to break
into the latter rounds. Usually, the preliminary
rounds are referred to as prelims, and later rounds
are referred to as elims, which is short for elimination rounds. Elimination rounds are also known as
outrounds.

After all the rounds are completed, there will
be an awards ceremony to recognize the winners. In
addition to awards for the top finishers in each event,
there are often sweepstakes awards for the best
overall speaker and the best overall club or school.
The final thing you will receive from a tournament
are the ballots which your judges have filled out for
you. These will be very helpful in providing construc-
tive comments which will give you advice to improve
your communication for the next time.

The Judges

Judges at individual events tournaments could
be just about any adult. Judges are usually parents
of competitors, other individuals from the community,
speech coaches, college students, and former competitors. At most tournaments you are expected to
provide a judge. This should be one of your parents
or another adult whom you know well. The judge
brought by you will not be assigned to judge you,
and in general you should not be judged by any one

whom you know very well. While some judges may have years of experience with competitive speech and forensics, the majority will be relatively inexperienced. These are known as lay judges, and you should be especially grateful to them for being willing to offer their free time to enable the tournament to happen. One of the most exciting aspects of competing in individual events is that you learn to communicate to a wide variety of audiences and people from all different backgrounds.

Judges will be judging you based on the general criteria for effective speaking, as seen in the categories on an individual events ballot. Before going to a competition you should always familiarize yourself with the ballot and the rules for your event so that you know exactly what judges are being instructed to look for. The bottom line is that every judge will reward the students who are most able to speak to that judge and communicate clearly and directly. Judging individual events can be remarkably subjective, and you will often find that the three judges in the round had very different reactions to your speech. In general, however, the best speakers are those who can rise above this and achieve the goal of communicating with anybody.

Tournament Dress and Appearance

Like it or not, an important part of communication is the way you present yourself, so you always want to dress well for a tournament. You want to project the image of a responsible, intelligent person who is worth listening to, so do not wear the same clothes you use to mow the lawn. Wear professional clothing which is clean and presentable. Avoid wearing anything immodest or that could possibly distract from your message, advice which is especially important for young ladies.

In addition to dressing appropriately, you should pay attention to other aspects of your personal appearance which may have an impact on how you are received by your audience. One of the most common mistakes made by competitors, both guys and girls, is to wear the hair hanging over the face. This will cause you to be constantly playing with it during your speech, as well as blocking out the most expressive part of your entire body, your eyes and eyebrows. Keep hair well groomed and off your face. Also eliminate gaudy or showy jewelry, excessive makeup, and pagers or cellular phones. It is not enough to turn these off, although that is obviously important. You should never have your pager or phone visible while speaking; it sends a bad message and is another source of distraction for the audience. Always bear in mind that it is very difficult for anyone to stay focused on one thing for ten minutes, regardless of how interesting you are, so cut down on every distraction within your power.

Tournament Etiquette

Christian speech tournaments are intended to improve students' abilities to think, speak, and present themselves in a Christian manner, and that is a goal that goes far beyond the actual act of speaking. You should always strive for Christlike attitudes toward fellow competitors, tournament coordinators, and judges. Think positive and concentrate on doing your best, not complaining if something goes wrong. If you always enter a tournament with this attitude you will make more friends, make a better impression on those around you, and have a much better experience than otherwise.

A general rule for handling yourself at a tournament is to treat others the same way that you expect to be treated. This means that you should never do things like talk or laugh loudly in hallways when people are speaking in the rooms, and never enter a room during some one's speech under any circumstances. When you are listening to another competitor in a round, pay attention and look at the speaker. Laugh when appropriate and clap at the end. Never use the time to review your own script, whisper to friends, or gaze out the window. You would not want someone else to do this during your speech, so you should not do it during someone else's speech. Watch and encourage the other speakers without doing anything to distract either them or the audience.

Be gracious and flexible when dealing with schedule or room changes, poor facilities, or special tournament conditions. Respect the facility where the tournament is being held, not abusing your privilege. The organizers of your tournament have done a lot of hard work, so be appreciative. They are probably very busy and stressed out, and the last thing they need to hear is your complaint. Never make disparaging remarks about other competitors, the facility, or the judges.

It is of special importance not to complain about the judges. No tournament would be possible without judges, and anyone who would be willing to sacrifice an entire day of their time to judge at a tournament is already doing you a huge favor. No judge is out to get you, or enjoys making speakers lose. Regardless of your opinion of a judge, never approach them to complain. Your personal contact with a judge should always be marked by respect, appreciation, and gratitude. If they approach you with specific comments, they are trying to help. Listen attentively, and learn from the observations they made about your presentation. On rare occasions, if you really believe that there is a problem with a judge, talk to your coach about it and let them handle the situation.

This attitude extends to your response to tournament results. If you do not break into outrounds, then go watch and support your teammates and friends who are still competing. When you do not win, congratulate those who did and compliment them on their success. Applaud the winners enthusiastically at the awards ceremony. When you do win, do not brag or show off, but receive your awards with grace and humility. These reactions are only possible when you are not obsessed with winning. The bottom line in any competition is that you should not base your personal happiness on whether you win or lose. That part is out of your hands, the only thing that you can control is ensuring that you do the very best job you possibly can.

Like all activities, public speaking cannot be learned overnight. Rather, it is a skill which you will need to persevere and work hard at in order to improve. As you begin to participate in competitive tournaments, it will probably take time before you achieve success. Work hard and aim high, but always temper this with a realization that the real purpose of the activity is to learn. Individual events tournaments are a great opportunity for education and fun, provided you pursue them with the right goals and attitudes.

Appendix B: Glossary

You may find yourself confused by some of the terms used at speech tournaments, or even some of the terms used in this book. The following is a short list of some of the most important public speaking words.

Advocacy: A speech intended to support a specific public policy proposal, in response to a social problem. This is a separate event in some speech leagues. In others, it is grouped together with Oratory or Persuasive Speaking.

Attention Getter: The opening words of a speech, designed to get the audience involved in the speech from the start.

Blocking: The movement used in an interpretation to bring literature to life. Blocking is especially important in duo interpretation.

Break: To qualify for the semifinal or final round at a speech tournament.

Character: A fictional person who is portrayed by the speaker in interpretation.

Character Profile: A written description of a character, used to help prepare for an interpretive speech.

Cutting: The script for any interpretive speech. It is called a cutting because the speaker usually cuts the script from a longer piece of literature.

Dramatic Interpretation: A memorized presentation of a serious fictional scene, intended to recreate a story without the use of properties, costumes, or anything extraneous to the body. Also called dramatic interp or D.I.

Duo Interpretation: A memorized presentation of a fictional scene, reenacted by two people.

Expository: A platform speech intended to inform the audience about a topic. Also called Expos.

Extemporaneous Speaking: A limited preparation speech about a current events topic. Also called extemp.

Extemp File: The box of research used to prepare an extemporaneous speech.

Extemp Prep Room: The room in which extemp competitors draw topics and prepare speeches, separate from the rooms where the speeches are actually delivered.

Eye Contact: Looking directly into the eyes of the audience.

Focal Point: Specific place in the room at which a speaker looks when portraying a character in an interpretation. Also called a point of reference.

Hook: Another word for the attention getter at the beginning of a speech.

Humorous Interpretation: A memorized presentation of a humorous fictional scene, intended to recreate a story without the use of properties, costumes, or anything extraneous to the body. Also called humorous interp or H.I.

Impromptu Speaking: A limited preparation speech prepared in the presence of the audience.

Interpretation: A performance of literature intended to evoke the meaning and feeling of the work being performed without the use of properties, costumes, or anything extraneous to the body.

Judge: The person who determines the winners in speech competition.

Limited Preparation Speech: A speech in which the speaker is given the topic a set amount of time before delivering the speech.

Manuscript: The word for word text of a speech.

Original Oratory: A platform speech intended for the edification or exhortation of the audience. Also called O.O.

Persuasive Speech: A speech intended to change the behavior or beliefs of the audience.

Piece: The work of literature used for an interpretation.

Platform Speech: Any speech written by the speaker.

Posting: The place where the schedule is displayed at a speech tournament. Includes information about where rounds are being held, who the judges are, and the order of speakers.

Qualifying Tournament: A tournament at which the winners earn the right to continue competing at a higher level, such as a state or national tournament.

Selection: The work of literature used for an interpretation.

Subtext: An analysis of an interpretive script, taking into account the thought, emotions, and motivations of each character.

Tab Room: The place where results are calculated at a speech tournament.

Thesis: A short statement that clearly explains the purpose of a speech.

Appendix C: Checklists and Critique Sheets

The following forms are for speech competitors. The checklists can be used to evaluate and improve speeches that are being prepared for competition. The critique sheets offer an easy tool for a coach or observer to judge the overall effectiveness of a presentation. You may photocopy and use these if you find them helpful in assessing and improving the quality of your students' speeches.

Oratory and Persuasive Checklist

No matter what your subject matter is, every original speech you deliver should have certain important features. Deliver your speech before an audience, and talk about whether or not your speech covered everything on this checklist. Discuss how you could make the speech flow better, and what little details you might be able to add.

1. Structure

____ How well do the introduction and conclusion fit together?

____ How well do the points of your speech flow? Do you sound like you are rambling at times (think about transitions)?

____ Is your thesis clear? Can your audience explain what your speech is about in one or two sentences?

2. Content

____ Does the audience find your speech convincing? What questions do they have and how could you deal with those in your speech?

____ Does your outline really support the point you want to make?

____ How well do you support your thesis? Do you use different kinds of evidence (statistics, illustrations, quotations)?

3. Interest

____ Is your speech interesting or boring? Are there parts that drag on?

____ Do you have any jokes? *Every* speech should have some humor.

____ What single point does the audience remember? Is that what you want them to remember?

4. Emotion

____ What emotion is your audience left with at the end of your speech? Is this what you want them to be feeling?

____ What are your emotional high points? Do you have a certain story that really grabs the audience?

____ How does your delivery work with your content?

Expository Checklist

No matter what your subject matter is, every expository speech you deliver should have certain important features. Deliver your speech before an audience, and talk about whether or not your speech covered everything on this checklist. Discuss how you could make the speech flow better, and what little details you might be able to add.

1. Structure

____ How well do the introduction and conclusion fit together?

____ How well do the points of your speech flow? Do you sound like you are rambling at times (think about transitions)?

____ Is your thesis clear? Can your audience explain what your speech is about in one or two sentences?

2. Content

____ Does the audience find your speech informative? Do you cover all the important aspects of your topic?

____ Do the facts you present fit into a recognizable outline?

____ How does your delivery work with your content? Do you present an appropriate level of animation and enthusiasm?

3. Interest

____ Is your speech interesting or boring? Are there parts that drag on?

____ Do you have any jokes? *Every* speech should have some humor.

____ What single point does the audience remember? Is that what you want them to remember?

4. Visual Aids

____ Do your visual aids enhance or distract from your presentation? Does each visual aid have a clear purpose and connection to your speech? Are they creative and eye-catching?

____ How do you handle your visual aids? Are you in control at all times?

____ Do your visual aids look nice and clean? Are they too cluttered or sloppy?

Extemporaneous Checklist

These are the elements of a successful extemporaneous speech. After practicing in front of an audience, talk about how well you accomplished these things. Think about what would have made the speech better, and how to incorporate all of these points.

1. Thesis

____ Did you answer your question?

____ Did the audience get the message?

____ How could you have made this more clear?

2. Introduction/Conclusion

____ How did you begin your speech? How did you end?

____ Does the audience remember your introduction and conclusion?

____ How well did this help to answer your question? Could you have tied it together better?

3. Outline

____ What were your major points? Did each point have an evidence source to back it up?

____ Did you make your outline clear? Does the audience remember it?

____ Did your outline points support your thesis? What would have made them better?

4. Evidence

____ Did you have evidence for each point? How many different sources did you use? How timely and authoritative were your sources?

____ Why did you choose this evidence? What purpose did it serve in your speech?

____ Was your evidence persuasive? Did you use different kinds of evidence (statistics, stories, quotations)?

Impromptu Checklist

Your impromptu speech should have certain features to be effective. After you have given your speech, you and your audience should be able to remember each of these things from your speech. Talk about the items on the checklist, whether you did every single one, and how each could have been done better.

1. Thesis
____ What was the point of your speech?

____ Did the audience get the message?

____ How could you have made this more clear?

2. Introduction/Conclusion
____ How did you begin your speech? How did you end?

____ Does the audience remember your introduction and conclusion?

____ How well did this tie into your main point? Could you have tied it together better?

3. Outline
____ What were your major points?

____ Did you make your outline clear? Does the audience remember it?

____ Did your outline points support your thesis? What would have made them better?

4. Stories and Illustrations
____ Did you use stories or illustrations for each point?

____ Why did you choose those illustrations? What purpose did they serve in your speech?

____ Did you tell your illustrations well? Did they hold the audience's attention? How could they have been made more interesting?

Dramatic Interpretation Checklist

You should practice your dramatic interpretation in front of an audience so that they can give you feedback. This checklist has some things to keep in mind. Discuss your speech, and think about how each of these things could be made better.

1. Script

____ Is the script easy to follow? Are there times when the audience is confused?

____ Are there times when the speech feels rushed? How does the script fit in the time limits?

____ Do you have any memorization problems?

____ Is your introduction clear and attention-getting?

2. Characters

____ Can the audience tell your characters apart? Do you tend to mix them up at any point in your speech?

____ Are the shifts between characters crisp or do they seem awkward?

____ What could you add to each character to make that character more fully convincing?

____ What change does each character undergo over the course of your speech? Does the audience catch this? Do you capture it fully?

3. Emotion

____ What is the emotional reaction of the audience? Is this what you thought your speech would accomplish?

____ Do any of your mannerisms distract from your emotional impact?

____ Does the audience believe you? Do your characters really seem to feel what is happening in the story?

Humorous Interpretation Checklist

You should practice your humorous interpretation in front of an audience so that they can give you feedback. This checklist has some things to keep in mind. Discuss your speech, and think about how each of these things could be made better.

1. Script

____ Is the script easy to follow? Are there times when the audience is confused?

____ Are there times when the speech feels rushed? How does the script fit in the time limits?

____ Do you have any memorization problems?

____ Is your introduction clear and attention-getting?

2. Characters

____ Can the audience tell your characters apart? Do you tend to mix them up at any point in your speech?

____ Are the shifts between characters crisp or do they seem awkward?

____ What could you add to each character to make that character more fully convincing? How could you make each character funnier?

____ What change does each character undergo over the course of your speech? Does the audience catch this? Do you capture it fully?

3. Humor

____ What parts does the audience laugh at? Is this what you thought your speech would accomplish?

____ Could you add facial expressions, reactions, or blocking to create more humor in your speech?

____ What is the source of comedy in this piece? How can you emphasize that further?

Duo Interpretation Checklist

You should practice your duo interpretation in front of an audience so that they can give you feedback. This checklist has some things to keep in mind. Discuss your speech, and think about how each of these things could be made better.

1. Script

____ Is the script easy to follow? Are there times when the audience is confused?

____ Are there times when the speech feels rushed? How does the script fit in the time limits?

____ Do you have any memorization problems?

____ Is your introduction clear and attention-getting?

2. Blocking

____ Do the two performers interact well with each other? Are your motions coordinated precisely?

____ Is there an even balance between performers?

____ What blocking could you add to enhance the lifelike quality of the inter-pretation?

____ Do both performers appear to be reacting to what the other is saying? Are you fully in character even when your partner is speaking?

3. Emotion

____ What is the emotional reaction of the audience? Is this what you thought your speech would accomplish?

____ Do any of your mannerisms distract from your emotional impact?

____ Does the audience believe you? Do your characters really seem to feel what is happening in the story?

Speech Critique Form   Name:_____
Platform Speeches   Topic:_____

Circle or Highlight Appropriate Comments

Introduction:

Don't start talking until you have everyone's attention; fails to command audience attention; needs more confidence and enthusiasm in the beginning; does not preview main points of speech; lacks a smooth transition from introduction to body.

Delivery:

A. <u>POSTURE</u>: Appears stiff, uncomfortable; rocks back and forth on feet; shuffles feet; needs to distribute weight evenly; avoid all weight on one leg.

B. <u>MOBILITY</u>: Needs to walk more during periods of transition; plant feet firmly after transitional movement; do not wander around during entire presentation.

C. <u>CONFIDENCE</u>: Smile and appear friendly (when appropriate); comes across as being too cocky, too self-assured; avoid nervous habits.

D. <u>GESTURES</u>: Keep hands at side when <u>not</u> gesturing; all gestures need to be above the waist; gestures too much with right/left hand only; gesture more with bboth hands simultaneously.

E. <u>PACE/VOCAL VARIETY</u>: Speaks too fast / too slow; needs to make more use of upper/lower registers of voice; speaks too loudly / too softly; speaks in a monotone; tends to slur words together.

F. <u>EYE CONTACT</u>: Doesn't make enough eye contact; looks too much at the floor/ at ceiling/ out the window/ above our head/ at the wall.

G. <u>MEMORIZATION</u>: We have the feeling you're reciting for us, not talking to us; major distraction such as long pause, apology, or embarrassed expression when line is dropped; has not memorized this speech; is paraphrasing own words.

H. <u>VISUAL AIDS (expos only)</u>: Not enough humor; not enough visual aids; aids not visual; aids too small; printing too small; clumsiness with visual aids detracts from presentation; chart stays up too long - audience is distracted. We're looking at <u>it</u> instead of you.

Content:

Lack of clear thesis or speech purpose; unclear outline structure; speaker fails to adequately defend points with evidence or example; no transitions from point to point.

Conclusion:

Unsatisfying or abrupt ending; needs to review reasoning and thesis; facial expression and body language convey dissatisfaction with own speech; returns to chair too quickly.

Overall Evaluation and Final Comments:

Speech Critique Form   Name:_____
Interpretive Speeches   Title:_____

Circle or Highlight Appropriate Comments

Introduction:

Introduction moves too slowly, fails to grab audience interest; does not clearly identify title and author.

_____

Delivery:

A. CHARACTERIZATION: Difficult to tell characters apart; slow and cumbersome transitions between characters; you tend to blend aspects of different characters together, especially towards the end.

B. VOICE: Voices seem strained or artificial; different characters have nearly identical voices; speaks too softly/loudly; speaks too fast/ too slow; character voices are inconsistent.

C. MEMORIZATION: Speech sounds too formal, like a recitation, not an interpretation; major distraction such as a long pause, apology, or embarrassed expression when line is dropped; has not memorized this piece; is paraphrasing author's words.

D. INTERPRETATION: Characters seem unbelievable, come across as caricatures or stereotypes; speaker tends to lapse in and out of character; lacks genuine feeling and emotion; interpretation moves too quickly, feels scripted and not spontaneous; speaker loses composure and laughs at script's lines (humorous only).

E. USE OF BODY: No focal points or focal points are inconsistent; posture does not seem to fit characters; posture changes between characters are slow and distracting; speaker makes eye contact with audience while in character; sways or steps back and forth.

_____

Selection:

Piece lacks sufficient literary merit, characters and scenes are shallow or unrealistic; cutting feels incomplete, not dramatically self-contained; too much intrusion by narrator (except in prose and poetry interpretation); selection contains inappropriate language or situations; scene is too complex and difficult to follow.

_____

Overall Evaluation and Final Comments:

Speech Critique Form   Name:_____
Limited Preparation Events   Topic:_____

Circle or Highlight Appropriate Comments

Introduction:

Don't start talking until you have everyone's attention; fails to command audience attention; needs more confidence and enthusiasm in the beginning; lacks a smooth transition from introduction to body; fails to preview main points of speech.

Delivery:

A. <u>POSTURE</u>: Appears stiff, uncomfortable; rocks back and forth on feet; shuffles feet; needs to distribute weight evenly; avoid all weight on one leg.

B. <u>MOBILITY</u>: Needs to walk more during periods of transition; plant feet firmly after transitional movement; do not wander around during entire presentation.

C. <u>CONFIDENCE</u>: Smile and appear friendly (when appropriate); comes across as being too cocky, too self-assured; avoid nervous habits.

D. <u>GESTURES</u>: Keep hands at side when <u>not</u> gesturing; all gestures need to be above the waist; gestures too much with right/left hand only; gesture more with both hands simultaneously.

E. <u>PACE/VOCAL VARIETY</u>: Speaks too fast / too slow; needs to make more use of upper/lower registers of voice; speaks too loudly / too softly; speaks in a monotone; tends to slur words together.

F. <u>EYE CONTACT</u>: Doesn't make enough eye contact; looks too much at the floor/ at ceiling/ out the window/ above our head/ at the wall.

G. <u>FLUENCY</u>: Long pauses while you try to find your thoughts; you say "um" and "uh" frequently; tendency to trip over words and get tongue-tied, often because you are speaking too quickly.

Content:

Lack of clear thesis or speech purpose; unclear outline structure; speaker fails to adequately defend points with evidence or example; no transitions from point to point; appears to be rambling and fails to tie speech together; speaker does not appear to comprehend topic fully; does not adequately address topic..

Conclusion:

Unsatisfying or abrupt ending; needs to review reasoning and thesis; facial expression and body language convey dissatisfaction with own speech.

Overall Evaluation and Final Comments:

Acknowledgements

I would first like to thank my parents for being amazingly loving and accommodating through the crazy process of putting this book together. My dad is the public speaker who has influenced me the most, and I seek to emulate his passion for communicating God's truths to the world. My mom is a tireless encourager as well as a perceptive critic. Her editing made this book possible.

Many teachers and coaches have helped me to learn the tools of public speaking. Mr. James Harville first introduce me to public speaking in a high school rhetoric class, and Chris Wolf, Kim Jones, and Dave Callaway have all inspired and taught me along the way. This book also uses some of the theories that are presented in the instructional videos of Ron Krikac, professor of forensics at Bradley University. More than any other instructor, Teresa Moon has encouraged and worked with me, always spurring me to be first and foremost a communicator for Christ.

Without God, none of this would be possible, and without God, none of this would be worth doing. I pray that He uses this book as just a small part of His plan to reach the world through His people.

About the Author

Thane Rehn has been competing in forensics for over eight years. In high school, he won several national awards in both speech and debate, including a national championship in extemporaneous speaking through the American Association of Christian Schools. Thane spent a year on tour as a conference instructor with Communicators for Christ and has coached many individual events competitors, including several national champions. He now coaches debate through the Urban Debate League in a public school in Chicago.

In 2002, Thane finished in fourth place at the national tournament of the American Parliamentary Debate Association. He is currently pursuing his studies at the University of Chicago, where he is the publisher of the student newspaper.